ROLLS - ROYCE HERITAGE TRUST

GW01459080

OLYMPUS

—the first forty years

Alan Baxter

HISTORICAL SERIES No 15

Published in 1990 by the
Rolls-Royce Heritage Trust
PO Box 31 Derby England

ISBN: 1-9511710-9-7

The Historical Series is published as a joint venture by the
Rolls-Royce Heritage Trust and the Sir Henry Royce memorial Foundation.

Also published in the series:

No. 1 Rolls-Royce—the formative years, 1906-1939
       Alec Harvey-Bailey, published by RRHT
No. 2 The Merlin in Perspective—the combat years
       Alec Harvey-Bailey, published by RRHT
No. 3 Rolls-Royce—the pursuit of excellence
       Alec Harvey-Bailey and Mike Evans, published by HRMF
No. 4 In the Beginning—the Manchester origins of Rolls-Royce
       Mike Evans, published by RRHT
No. 5 Rolls-Royce—the Derby Bentleys
       Alec Harvey-Bailey, published by HRMF
No. 6 The Early Days of Rolls-Royce—and the Montagu Family
       Lord Montagu of Beaulieu, published by RRHT
No. 7 Rolls-Royce—Hives, The Quiet Tiger
       Alec Harvey-Bailey, published by HRMF
No. 8 Rolls-Royce—Twenty to Wraith
       Alec Harvey Bailey, published by HRMF
No. 9 Rolls-Royce and the Mustang
       David Birch, published by RRHT
No. 10 From Gipsy to Gem—With diversions
       Peter Stokes, published by RRHT
No. 11 Armstrong Siddeley—the Parkside story, 1896-1939
       Ray Cook, published by RRHT
No. 12 Henry Royce—mechanic
       Donald Bastow, published by RRHT
No. 14 Rolls-Royce—the Sons of Martha
       Alec Harvey-Bailey, published by HRMF

Cover Photo This view of 'Alpha Alpha' shows to advantage the location of the engine nacelles
and the graceful shape of the slender delta wing.   [*British Aerospace*]

Printed by Bemrose Security Printing, Derby

OLYMPUS - The first forty years

Contents

Chapter 1	Early Development	10
Chapter 2	Vulcan	40
Chapter 3	TSR2	76
Chapter 4	Industrial and Marine	100
Chapter 5	Concorde	131

Glossary

Appendix 1	Olympus Powered Aircraft Proposals	172
Appendix 2	Olympus Family Tree	173
Appendix 3	How the Jet Engine Works	176

| Bibliography | | 179 |

PREFACE

The first engine that I worked on when I joined the Bristol Aeroplane Company in 1952 was an early version of the Olympus two-spool axial flow jet engine, and I was also involved with many of its subsequent developments including the Olympus 593.

On retiring from Rolls-Royce some 37 years later as Director Military Engines, the Olympus 593 engine in Concorde remains the most powerful turbojet engine in service. The story so ably told in the pages that follow is not only that of a particular engine series but also of the determined response of Bristol to the engineering and business challenges of the gas turbine.

J D Wragg
December 1989

FOREWORD

The Olympus was key to the survival and prosperity of Bristol Engines.

In 1945, having been late in entering the gas turbine field, the small Bristol team was busy with the Theseus and Proteus turboprops. In May of that year Frank Owner saw an opportunity to contest the main stream jet engine market, and set the three-man project office the task of designing a 9000lb thrust two-spool jet engine. It was a visionary act on his part in circumstances that were not obviously conducive to success, with an ambitious project to be undertaken by a relatively inexperienced and heavily committed team.

Rig test results were beginning to appear when Stanley Hooker came to Bristol, and under his leadership progress was rapid. The adoption of Olympus for the Vulcan bomber and the subsequent defence of this position against a variety of attacks ensured the continuation of engine activity at Bristol.

The original design was necessarily conservative, based as it was on the sparse data base available in 1945 and involving the minimum of technical adventures. Although the team was small, or more likely because of this fact, the design was well balanced with ample scope for future development.

These characteristics enabled supersonic derivatives to compete successfully for TSR2 and Concorde, and the engine proved suitable for power generation and marine propulsion. The Olympus core was the basis of the BS100 vectored thrust engine for the Hawker P1154, and scaled down was the heart of the M-45 series of engines.

Thus by the 60s a strong position had been established ensuring the continuation of gas turbine engineering at Bristol into the next century.

In the aero engine business development is the name of the game, and the evolution of the Olympus to the standards required by Concorde was achieved by the dedicated attention of many engineers of all disciplines. The story of Olympus development is told by Alan Baxter, partly from painstaking research but also from memory for he has made his own contribution to this endeavour.

It is a story of overall success, punctuated by mysteries, disappointments, failures and disasters, the challenges accepted and resolved by development engineering.

Gordon Lewis
President of Bristol branch of RRHT
December 1989.

AUTHOR'S NOTE

I first encountered the Olympus just two weeks after I joined the Flight Test Department of Bristol Siddeley Engines Limited in February 1961. Charles Harding, the Chief Flight Test Engineer, appeared in front of my desk and asked me if I had my bag with me.

"Bag? What bag, Charles." I asked.

"Your overnight bag. You're off to Woodford this afternoon." was the reply.

So, in company with Dick Elder, a senior flight test engineer, I found myself heading north up the A38 that afternoon to Woodford, in Cheshire, where A.V.Roe and Company had their Vulcan production line and flight test facility. At the time, Vulcan B2s powered by the Olympus 201 were just entering service and were encountering engine handling problems. One aircraft had been returned from the RAF because of these problems, hence our hurried departure from Patchway.

That visit to Woodford, albeit made in a state of total ignorance about jet engines as far as I was concerned, marked the start of nearly twenty years association with the Olympus, as later I worked on the Mark 320 for TSR2, the Mark 301 for the Vulcan B2 and the Mark 593 for Concorde.

This book grew out of an attempt to write down the highlights of a largely uneventful test flying career. During this attempt it became apparent that the story of the Olympus was far more interesting than my somewhat mundane experiences. So the focus of the narrative changed, to become a semi-technical history of the development and operational use, in all its varied applications, of what was to become the Western world's most powerful production turbojet.

The Olympus started life as a brilliantly innovative design from the Turbine Department of the Aero-Engine Division of the Bristol Aeroplane Company, and it was progressively developed, initially for the Vulcan four-jet bomber. The acceptance by the Ministry of Defence of the Bristol submission for the engine to power the TSR2 led to the merger with Armstrong Siddeley Motors Limited (ASM) of Coventry, in 1959 to form Bristol Siddeley Engines Limited (BSEL). Also from about 1959 the Armstrong Siddeley plant at Ansty, near Coventry, was engaged in overhauling early marks of Olympus, and it later became the centre for industrial and marine applications of aviation gas turbines, roles which provided separate lines of development for the Olympus.

In turn, BSEL was acquired by Rolls-Royce in 1966, becoming the Bristol Engine Division. 1966 marked the first flight of the Olympus 593, slung underneath a Vulcan flying test bed. Many of the activities on the Olympus occurred in parallel, and I have consequently used the company name that was in use at the time. Thus one can find references to Bristol, BSEL and Rolls-Royce scattered apparently at random throughout these pages.

Many people have assisted me in preparing this work, and to those who are too numerous to name I extend my grateful thanks. The Bristol branch of the Rolls-Royce

8

Heritage Trust (RRHT) very kindly allowed me unrestricted access to their library, and committee member John Heaven was indefatigable in unearthing fresh facts and documents that I had missed, as well as putting me right on many aspects of Olympus development. I also owe a great deal to the enthusiasm and support of the Bristol branch Chairman, Philip Christie, who urged me on when the going was difficult, and to Mike Evans, the RRHT Chairman, for his encouragement and constructive comments on my first draft.

My thanks are also due to Gordon Lewis, President of the Bristol branch of the RRHT, John Wragg who retired last year as Director, Military Engines, and Ralph Denning, who were kind enough to review this book. Their vast experience of all aspects of Olympus development caused me considerable anxiety as I awaited their comments, but it will come as no surprise to their colleagues to find that they were very kind, and made many helpful suggestions that shed light on several events that would otherwise have remained obscure.

The Press Offices at Bristol and Ansty were very tolerant of my continual requests for information and photographs, and the Photographic Department at Patchway must have spent many hours sorting through old negatives. To the staffs of all these departments I offer my sincere thanks; this book would have been the poorer without their efforts.

In writing this story, I have sometimes had to reconcile conflicting accounts. Any misinterpretations or errors resulting from this or any other cause are mine alone.

This book was written to mark the 40th Anniversary of the first test bed run of the Olympus. I look forward to producing a revised edition for the Golden Anniversary, in the year 2000. To that end I would be grateful for any criticisms or corrections to the material contained herein, and especially for any additional information that would enable the story of the Olympus to be completed.

It may be that some readers of this book will be unfamiliar with the way in which a jet engine works. Appendix Three contains a simplified description of the principles which govern the operation of a jet engine. It was produced by Rolls-Royce for non-technical readers, and if read first will add greatly to the book's enjoyment.

The use of some technical terms is unavoidable in a work such as this, although I have tried to keep their use to the minimum; the explanation of those that do occur can be found in the glossary.

Alan Baxter
Flight Test Department
March 1990.

1. Early Development

When the Olympus jet engine was first designed, it was intended to power bomber aircraft capable of achieving 500 mph and 40,000 feet. Its designers would have been astonished if they had known then that forty years on, much developed versions would power the World's only successful supersonic transport, warships of many navies and in addition would be used to generate electrical power sometimes in remote and inhospitable areas. Moreover, in all these aspects the Olympus would bid fair to continue in use to beyond the end of the century. From the outset it was intended that the engine would have the potential for significant increases in thrust, but it is most unlikely that anyone could have envisaged a thrust growth from the initial 9,140 lb of the Olympus B.01.1 to the 38,000 lb of the Olympus 593-610 in Concorde. This success story is all the more surprising when it is realised that the Olympus was Bristol's first serious venture into the field of jet propulsion, and was initially conceived during a period when actual running experience in the Company was virtually non-existent.

The first assessment of the gas turbine as a potential aero-engine was made by Frank Owner in 1924. He considered its use in turbo-prop form as a replacement for the piston engine, and with Roy Fedden came to the conclusion that with the materials and knowledge available, such a device would produce less power, and burn more fuel, than its rival. Much later, in March 1931, Frank Whittle went to see Roy Fedden in order to describe his ideas on jet propulsion. At Fedden's request Owner studied the proposals and reported that the theory was sound and would undoubtedly come to fruition, but not for about ten years. He told Fedden that 'it wouldn't pull the skin off a rice pudding.', a phrase which Fedden became fond of quoting. Fedden, RF as he was known by his staff, knew that with a new family of sleeve-valve engines under development, Bristol did not have the resources to give to the gas turbine the effort it would undoubtedly require. It was also evident at the time that the gas turbine would offer no real competition to the piston engine for some years to come, particularly as far as fuel consumption was concerned.

In the late thirties major differences occurred between RF and the Board of Directors of the Bristol Aeroplane Company, the parent company of the Aero Engine Division that he had been largely instrumental in forming nearly twenty years earlier. By 1942 the rift had widened to the point where RF could no longer remain as Chief Engineer, and he reluctantly left. This was a shattering event, as he had dominated engine design and development at Bristol for more than two decades. However, under Frank Owner's direction, Bristol was about to take its first tentative steps into the gas turbine era, and the initial impetus came from outside.

In November 1941 Frank Owner was admitted to the second meeting of the Gas Turbine Collaboration Committee. He was quickly made aware of the number and variety of jet engines that were being designed, and it became clear that Bristol had little chance of adding to their number. It also appeared that Bristol's background in the design of engines for bomber and transport aircraft made a propeller turbine, or turbo-prop, a more logical choice than a jet engine. Such a choice also had the extra advantage that the jet-prop configuration did not feature in any of the other proposals.

An initial design for a turbo-prop of 4,000 shp received approval from the Ministry of Aircraft Production in April 1943. Out of this grew a more modest proposal for an engine with a rating of 2,000 shp which became the Theseus. The Ministry was very supportive of the project, the only caveat being that war production was not to be affected. As a consequence the early detail drawings were done by a team of apprentices

A proud history

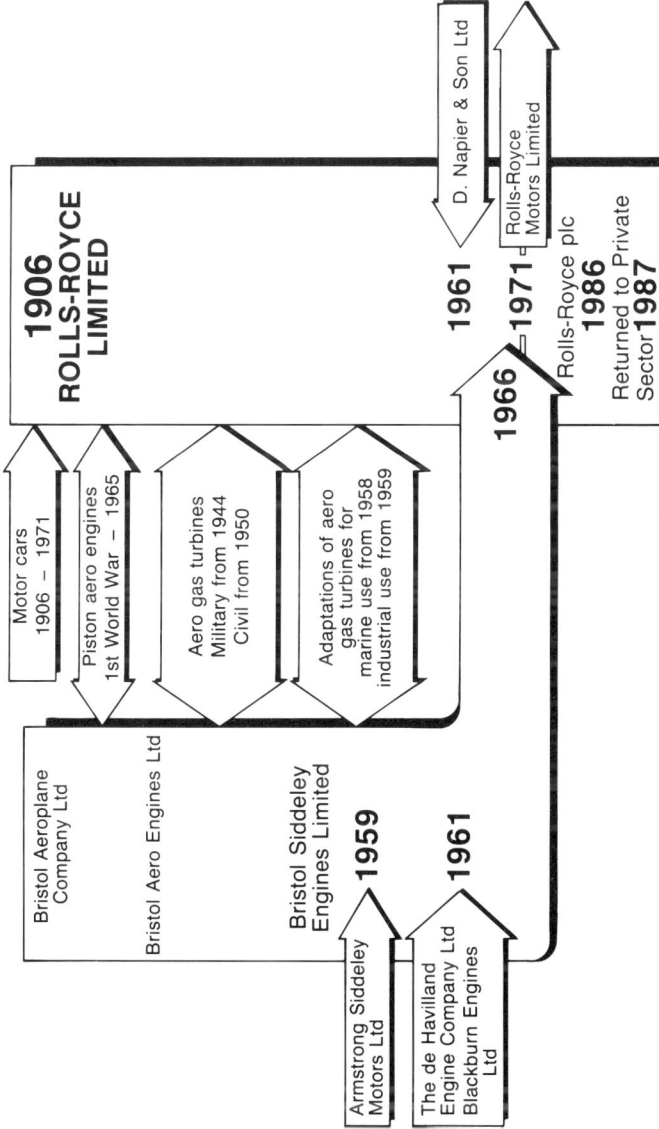

ROLLS ROYCE

1906
ROLLS-ROYCE LIMITED

Motor cars 1906 – 1971

Piston aero engines 1st World War – 1965

Aero gas turbines Military from 1944 Civil from 1950

Adaptations of aero gas turbines for marine use from 1958 industrial use from 1959

Bristol Aeroplane Company Ltd

Bristol Aero Engines Ltd

Bristol Siddeley Engines Limited **1959**

1961

Armstrong Siddeley Motors Ltd

The de Havilland Engine Company Ltd

Blackburn Engines Ltd

1961 D. Napier & Son Ltd

1971 Rolls-Royce Motors Limited

1966

Rolls-Royce plc **1986**

Returned to Private Sector **1987**

DMN

1303 B

The history of Rolls-Royce, showing the way in which the various engine firms amalgated to form the Company in its present form. [*Rolls-Royce*]

AXIAL COMPRESSOR   COMPRESSOR SHAFT   MOUNTING BEAM   COMPRESSOR TURBINE WHEEL   PROPELLER TURBINE WHEEL   HEAT EXCHANGER

AUXILIARY GEAR CASING   CENTRIFUGAL IMPELLER   TURBINE MOUNTING

AIR INTAKE

REDUCTION GEAR

PROPELLER SHAFT

ENGINE MOUNTING

TRANSFER PIPE

COMBUSTION CHAMBER

DIFFUSER

PROPELLER TURBINE SHAFT

STARTER MOTOR MOUNTING FACE

OIL PUMP DRIVE

OIL SUMP

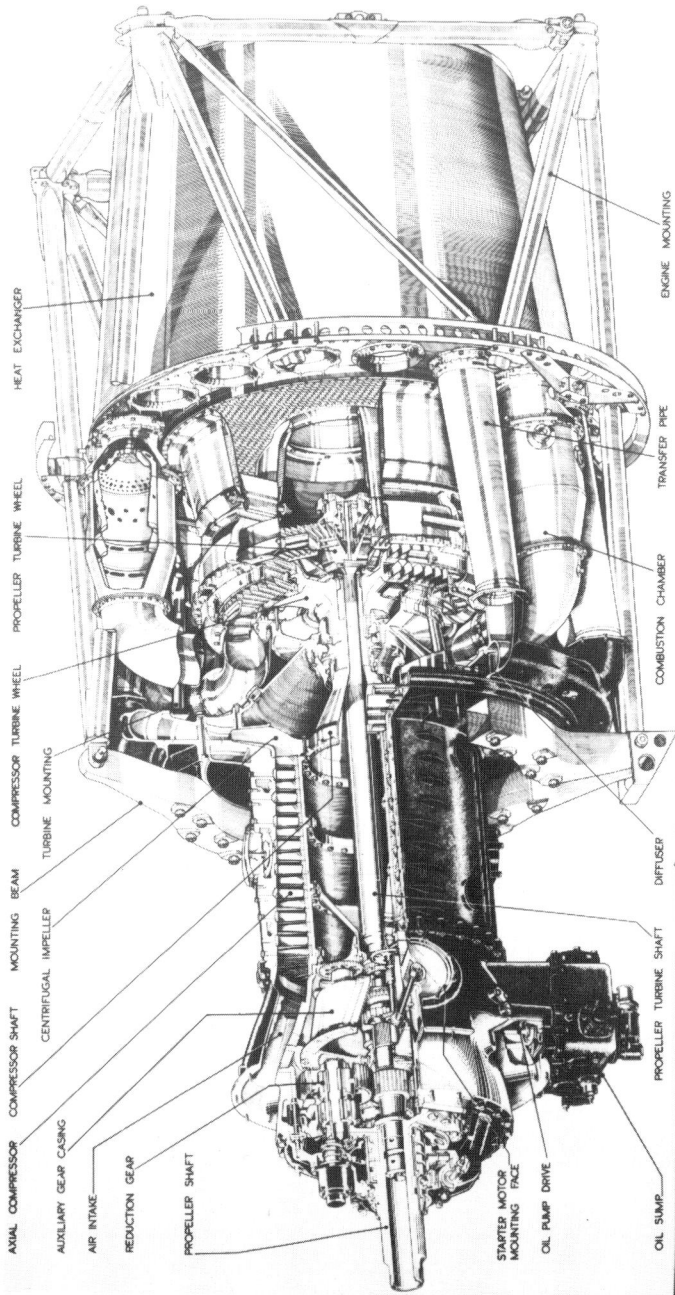

TECH PUBS D.O APRIL 1946

13382

"*Bristol*" THESEUS PROPELLER TURBINE

[*Rolls-Royce*]

The Bristol Theseus propeller turbine. This engine flew in the outboard nacelles of an Avro Lincoln in 1947, and subsequently powered the Handley Page Hermes V airliner, only two examples of which flew.

12

and trainees under the part-time guidance of more senior designers. This work was not carried out at Patchway, but at Tockington Manor, a country house some miles away from the main factory, a move designed to minimise the effects of enemy bombing raids.

The engine division at Patchway was situated on the opposite side of Filton Airfield from the aircraft works. It had grown in size since RF had selected the site, and had spread across the A38, the main Bristol to Gloucester Road, to occupy five large assembly sheds alongside a minor road known as Gipsy Patch Lane. During the war the engine works were heavily involved in the production of piston engines, with the bulk of the effort concentrated upon the Hercules sleeve-valve engine. Consequently by 1946, when the first speculative layouts of what was to become the Olympus were started, Bristol had no pure-jet operating experience whatsoever.

The Theseus flew for the first time in the outboard nacelles of a converted Lincoln bomber on 17 February 1947, and went on to power two examples of the Handley Page Hermes V. The engine did not go into quantity production as the design of a new engine, the Proteus, was commenced in November 1944. Although a turbo-prop, the Proteus offered the possibility of gaining some early pure-jet operating experience, as it was possible to easily manufacture a small jet engine based upon the gas generator section. The engine, named Phoebus, was capable of providing a useful 2,600 lb of thrust at a modest fuel consumption, and first ran on the test bed in June 1946.

By the end of that year only 10 hours operation had been achieved, whilst elsewhere experience was counted in the thousands. Even by the end of 1947 pure-jet running at Bristol only amounted to 180 hours, which included 27 hours in another converted Lincoln bomber.

In 1946 the Project Office was run by Charles Marchant who had a staff of two, designer Sam Robinson and a young graduate engineer, Gordon Lewis. In April of that year Frank Owner asked the Project Office to produce a design for a large jet engine. His brief included the definition of a compound, or two-spool, arrangement with a centrifugal high-pressure stage. Schemes were prepared by Marchant and Robinson, whilst Lewis calculated the effects of pressure ratio and turbine temperature and embarked upon the specification of the turbines and compressors.

An assessment of the likely performance that would be required of future bomber aircraft showed that speeds of the order of 600 mph at high altitude would be expected, and information from the Aircraft Division showed that the corresponding thrust required would be 7,000 lb per engine, assuming four per aircraft. At the prevailing levels of engine efficiency that was a very difficult target to achieve, and a number of alternatives using a large number of smaller engines were examined. One proposal used ten engines each producing 3,500 lb thrust.

It seemed logical that heavy bombers would require a greater increase in speed than transport aircraft, and that a jet engine would be required if the speed was to be of the order of 600 mph, a figure which progress in fighter aircraft indicated would be necessary. Long range—essential for a heavy bomber—suggested emphasis on fuel economy rather than low weight, and in a jet engine this meant high compression ratios and a moderate combustion temperature. The ability of aircraft designs to grow in weight as time passed was also well understood, so Owner decided to initially produce an engine with 9,000 lb thrust, and to investigate ways of increasing that to 12,000 lb by the time the extra power was needed.

As a result of these deliberations, a thrust target of 9,000 lb was defined, to be achieved using a compressor pressure ratio of 9 to 1. The highest pressure ratio attained

14/764

Avro Lincoln RA643, showing the Bristol Phoebus installation in the bomb bay. Only 23 flying hours were completed in this aircraft, which was the first pure jet installation carried out at Patchway.

[*Rolls-Royce*]

14

A close-up view of the Phoebus installation with the engine bay doors open.   [*Rolls-Royce*]

at that time was 5.5 to 1 in the Armstrong Siddeley Python turbo-prop engine. The Python had a single axial flow compressor which required 14 rows of blades, or stages, to obtain the desired compression, and suffered from slow acceleration rates because of its large size and poor surge margin. The decision by Frank Owner to aim at a value nearly double that of contemporaneous engines was a very courageous step indeed.

Experience of existing jet engines suggested that a pressure ratio of 9 to 1 could not be achieved using a single compressor without making unacceptable compromises in its flexibility of operation, whereas a two-shaft design with the compressors in series offered the possibility of achieving all the design aims, albeit at the expense of increased mechanical complexity. The new layout was known as a split compressor, and enabled the desired pressure ratio to be attained in two more manageable steps whilst at the same time providing faster accelerations. In addition the self-matching characteristics of two independently driven compressors would provide the prospect of reasonably surge free operation over a wide range of flight conditions.

The initial configuration considered had a ten-stage axial flow low pressure section followed by a centrifugal flow high pressure unit, the latter being chosen for its efficiency and resistance to surge. Each was driven by a single-stage turbine. The axial compressor was to have a pressure ratio of 5 to 1 which was in line with contemporary experience, and the centrifugal component would provide a further 1.8 to 1, giving 9 to 1 overall. This layout produced a number of problems. The diameter of the centrifugal compressor was 48 inches, considerably greater than the design target of 40 inches, and much worse, the centrifugal section had to rotate very fast in order to achieve the desired output. As a consequence the high pressure turbine was much smaller, and did far less work, than the low-revving low-pressure turbine. Increasing the number of low pressure stages to two, in an attempt to reduce its diameter, failed to resolve the turbine diameter incompatibility between the high and low pressure stages.

The next step was to put a small number of axial stages - three or four - in front of the centrifugal section to form a compound compressor. This made it possible to increase the diameter of the high pressure turbine and so obtain better overall turbine geometry. Unfortunately, fitting axial stages in this manner tended to reduce the efficiency of the centrifugal compressor, and as it was then producing only a fraction of its intended output, the case in its favour had almost disappeared, whereas the case for eliminating it was as strong as ever.

By November 1946 the results of Gordon Lewis's calculations indicated the superiority of the twin-axial arrangement, but Owner was still very keen on retaining the centrifugal high-pressure stage. However, the Director of Engine Research and Development (DEngRD) at the Ministry of Supply, Captain Maurice Luby, showed a favourable interest in the twin-axial layout, and with that Owner dropped his insistence on including a centrifugal component.

Once the decision had been taken to delete the centrifugal component, a fresh start could be made. Preliminary studies indicated that by choosing the correct split of pressure ratio between the compressors it would be possible to balance the work between the turbines in such a manner that only two turbine stages would be needed. The pressure ratios that were finally chosen were 2.7 to 1 for the low pressure, and 3.3 to 1 for the high-pressure compressors. This particular division had the advantage that the surge margins of each compressor were also similar at full and reduced power conditions, which augured well for the declared aim of excellent handling.

Whilst the early engine design studies were being made, the Aircraft Division of the Bristol Aeroplane Company was considering a long-range, high-flying bomber

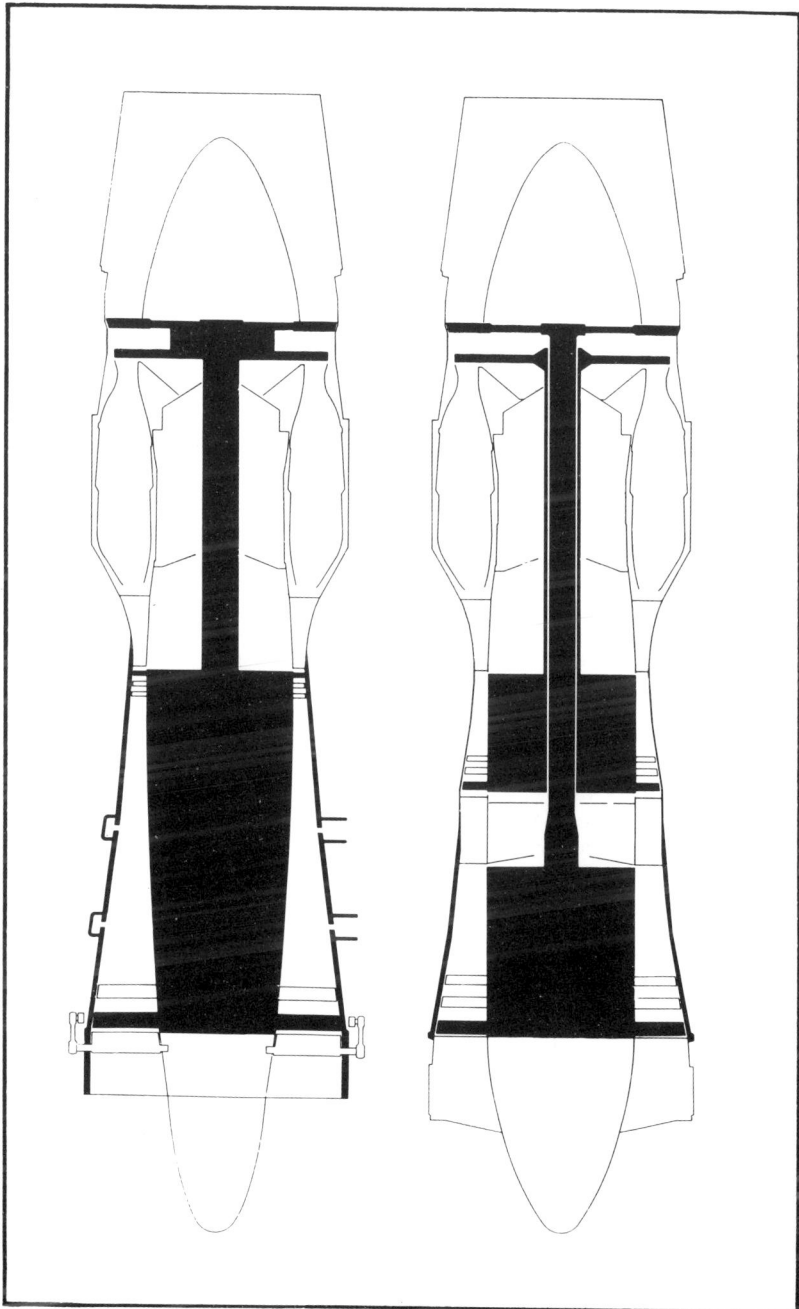

The two-spool layout compared to a single-spool. It offered higher compression ratios and lower fuel consumption at the cost of extra weight and complexity. [Rolls-Royce]

designated Type 172, that was to be powered by four Bristol turbojets of 9,000 lb thrust. These could only have been Olympus engines, as no other engine of comparable size was under development at Patchway at that time. The general specification of the Type 172 was the same Ministry of Supply specification that was later responsible for the Vulcan and Victor. With a crew of four the bomber would have achieved 600 mph at 50,000 feet and had a range of 5,400 miles.

The Filton bomber was abandoned by 1948, and work on the Olympus proceeded slowly as a result of factors outside the control of the designers. The main reason was the fact that the only other application of the engine was the Avro Vulcan, which was regarded as a rather long term project. As a result work which perhaps could have been compressed into two years was spaced over three.

The first twin spool configuration considered once the centrifugal stage had been dropped had seven low-pressure and eight high-pressure stages, each driven by a single stage turbine. This gradually evolved into the first BE 10, which had six low-pressure and eight high-pressure stages and which retained the single stage turbines. Combustion was to be achieved using a 'cannular' system, which had ten flame tubes connected together in a circular form. Two of these were fitted with high energy igniter plugs.

As far as can be determined, the Olympus was the first application of such a combustion chamber arrangement. The cannular system was chosen to keep the overall powerplant diameter within the 40 inch limit. It was realised that separate flame tubes would have increased the diameter beyond 40 inches, whilst a truly annular system was beyond the available technology.

With the foregoing decisions as a basis the Project Office prepared a brochure which was submitted to the Ministry of Supply in March 1946, and in July of that year the TE1/46 engine specification was issued. The brochure not only defined the basic engine but also briefly discussed thrust augmentation using reheat, and the possibility of boundary layer control using ducted fans. The board authorised the submission of a tender for six experimental engines to be manufactured to the specification and it was submitted at the end of January 1947.

In January 1949 Dr. S.G. Hooker joined Bristol from Rolls-Royce Derby. Dr. - later Sir Stanley - Hooker, SGH as he was sometimes known from his Derby reference, soon became aware that the main engine development effort was being expended on the Centaurus, and that there were too few engineers working on turbine development. There was a distinct attitude amongst some senior engineers that 'the turbine job' would never get anywhere. In about mid-1950, SGH was given the opportunity to do something about this state of affairs, as problems with the early Proteus led Norman Rowbotham, the Managing Director, to appoint him as Chief Engineer in place of Frank Owner. Shortly after this Owner left Bristol to join the de Havilland Engine Company. SGH lost no time in re-organising the turbine department, appointing Charles Marchant as Chief Engineer Turbine Engines and Neville Quinn as Chief of Research and Engine Performance. Later Basil Blackwell was recruited from Derby to look after turbine development, Gordon Lewis was put in charge of compressor design and performance, and Pierre Young, who was an ex-Armstrong Siddeley man, looked after overall engine performance. Young was to preside over the ultimate development of the Olympus, the 593 for the Anglo-French Concorde, for in mid-1966 he was appointed Chief Engineer and Programme Manager Olympus 593, a position for which he was uniquely qualified with his bi-lingual ability in English and French and his long association with the Olympus family.

18

Sir Stanley Hooker. 'SGH'.   [*Rolls-Royce*]

Partly because of the demise of the bomber project, manufacturing drawings were not issued to the experimental shops until January 1949, but thereafter progress was spectacular. Detailed design work was completed in seven months, and the first engine ran on 6 May 1950, only seventeen months after the first drawings were issued.

The first engine, designated B.01 1, weighed 3,600 lb and produced 9,140 lb thrust at a specific fuel consumption (sfc) of 0.83 lb/lb thrust/hour. Virtually no aerodynamic problems were encountered, and the standard of handling was considered a 'revelation' and set new standards of what handling should be.

The mechanical reliability was less impressive, as the problems that were experienced were structural in nature. One was particularly serious. Excessive deflection of a turbine diaphragm led to the LP compressor drive shaft being severed and the LP turbine disc ejected. It made a number of circuits around the test bed before coming to rest. Had the designers but known, it was not to be the last Olympus engine to do its best to demolish the test stand.

Subsequent engine development was rapid with the B.01 1/2 running on the test bed in November 1950 and producing a thrust of 9,500 lb. The B.01 1 was initially designed with provision for two starter motors, one for each spool; the early running showed that one starter to turn the HP spool was sufficient, and the B.01 1/2 and subsequent variants were designed with one only.

The B.01 1/2 had a single row of inlet guide vanes made of Hiduminium RR57 alloy. These had the novel feature of being adjustable for development running. Small protractors fitted outside the casing gave an accuracy of plus or minus a quarter of a degree, the set angle being of course locked during actual running.

The six-stage LP compressor was made from various light alloys within an L123 magnesium/zirconium casing split along the horizontal centre line. The eight-stage HP compressor was of all steel construction within a casing that was centrifugally cast in Firth Vickers FCB austenitic steel, again split along the horizontal centre line. The ten flame tubes were of Nimonic 75, each fitted with a Lucas duplex burner which injected downstream, and two interconnectors to carry the flame around from the two flame tubes fitted with high energy ignition units.

Both sets of HP and LP turbine blades were forged in Nimonic 80A, whereas the stator blades were cast in segments using Nimonic 80. The turbine blades were peen locked in fir tree serrations in discs of Rex 448 or Jessops H46 Ferritic steel. Both compressor shafts were forged out of S106 chrome-molybdenum steel.

The B.01 1/2A was very little different from the B.01 1, but was prepared to suit the needs of the Curtiss Wright Corporation of Woodridge, New Jersey. Several specimens of the B.01 1/2A were shipped over to the USA at a rating of 9,750 lb, and it was reported that on a cold New Jersey day a spot thrust figure of 10,000 lb was recorded. This was the first five figure thrust to be achieved by any British engine without thrust augmentation. As the TJ-32, it flew in a fixed nacelle under a B-29 test bed in 1951.

Curtiss Wright set their thrust target at 15,000 lb, and had the engine achieved that it would probably have been selected to power the Convair F102 all weather interceptor, with a US designation of J67. For some reason development could not push the thrust beyond the 12,000 lb mark, and no USAF orders were obtained.

With a bigger turbine and restaggered blades the engine became the B.01 1/2B which first ran in December 1951, and produced 9,750 lb thrust at an sfc of 0.766 lb/lb thrust/hr. Detail improvements on the 1/2B included relocation of all the accessory gear trains in the intermediate casing - they had previously been located in the delivery casing - and improvements in the combustion system. At Bristol the engine was getting

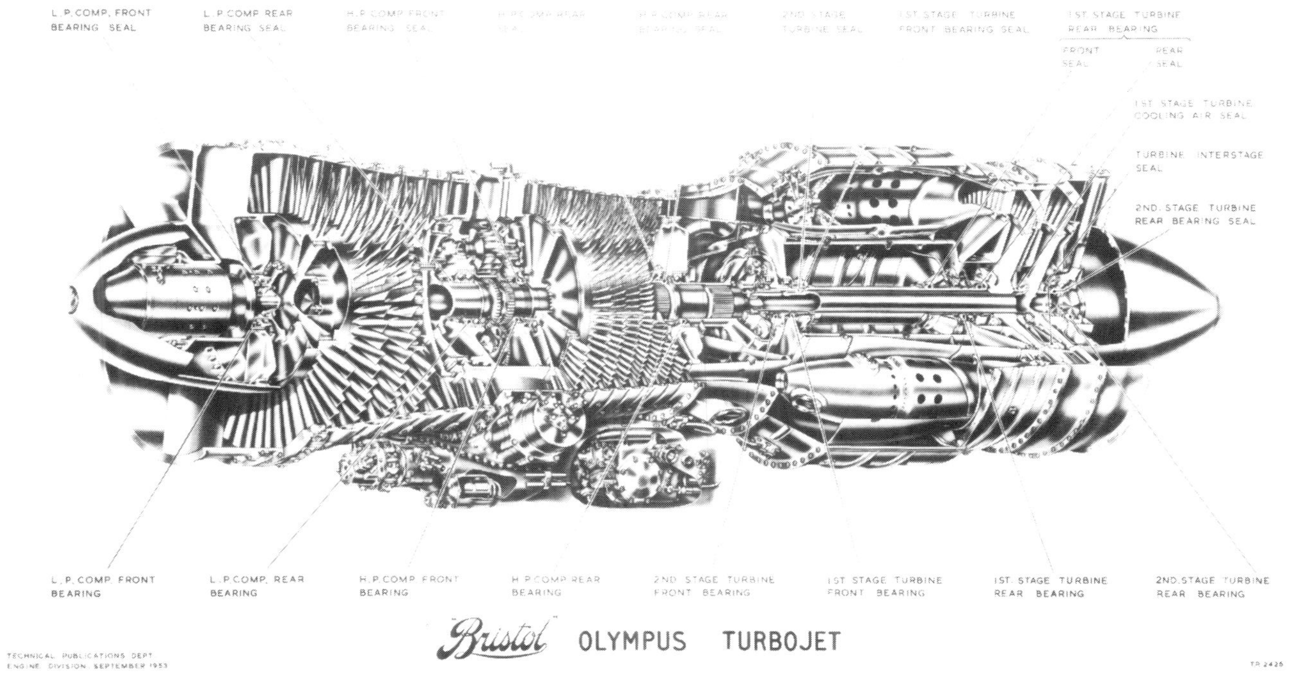

Bristol OLYMPUS TURBOJET

L P COMP FRONT BEARING SEAL

L P COMP REAR BEARING SEAL

H P COMP FRONT BEARING SEAL

H P COMP REAR BEARING SEAL

2ND STAGE TURBINE SEAL

1ST STAGE TURBINE FRONT BEARING SEAL

1ST STAGE TURBINE REAR BEARING

FRONT SEAL

REAR SEAL

1ST STAGE TURBINE COOLING AIR SEAL

TURBINE INTERSTAGE SEAL

2ND STAGE TURBINE REAR BEARING SEAL

L P COMP FRONT BEARING

L P COMP REAR BEARING

H P COMP FRONT BEARING

H P COMP REAR BEARING

2ND STAGE TURBINE FRONT BEARING

2ND STAGE TURBINE REAR BEARING

1ST STAGE TURBINE FRONT BEARING

1ST STAGE TURBINE REAR BEARING

2ND STAGE TURBINE REAR BEARING

TD 2425

TECHNICAL PUBLICATIONS DEPT.
ENGINE DIVISION SEPTEMBER 1953

A cutaway view of an Olympus Mark 101. It is instructive to compare this with the similar view of an Olympus Mark 551 shown later in this chapter.
[*Rolls-Royce*]

21

very close to the flight stage. With little modification it became the Olympus 99, and derated to 8,000 lb thrust largely owing to airframe limitations, two were fitted in a Canberra B2 in place of the original Avons.

The Lincolns that were used for early gas turbine flight development had performed well in introducing Bristol to the jet era, but it soon became apparent that the potential of the gas turbine far exceeded the capabilities of the converted piston engined bombers. What was needed was a modern high performance airframe designed to exploit the full potential of the gas turbine. The first of these arrived in the form of Canberra B2 WD952 in 1952.

Prior to and during the war, operational flying above 40,000 feet was something of a rarity, and was restricted largely to record breaking attempts and a few high flying reconnaissance aircraft. The gas turbine changed all that. It produced the fastest expansion of the flight envelope ever seen in the history of aviation. Flight above 40,000 feet became commonplace, and 60,000 feet was soon exceeded. Airspeeds increased even more dramatically, with the magic 1,000 mph being surpassed by the Fairey Delta 2 on 10 March 1956, piloted by Peter Twiss. Gas turbine powered aircraft penetrated into hitherto unexplored realms and new problems were not slow in appearing.

The specification for the V-bombers called for high speed flight at the highest possible altitudes, so it was natural that advantage was taken of the Olympus Canberra's performance to explore engine behaviour above 40,000 feet as soon as possible. As the Olympus B.01 1/2B provided virtually double the thrust of the original Avons, the aircraft became quite a hot rod. Its initial rate of climb was over 15,000 feet per minute, and it could exceed its critical Mach Number-about 0.8-on one engine at 50,000 feet. WD952 flew for the first time with Olympus engines fitted on 5 August 1952, the pilot being Wing Commander Walter Gibb,DSO,DFC.

After the first flight engine development followed along normal lines, with calibration and handling tests being carried out at all altitudes up to 60,000 feet. Several unexpected problems occurred during the initial high altitude flights. Performance measurements had shown that jet pipe temperatures were much higher than sea level calculations had predicted, and this led to much extensive witch hunting into thermocouples, cold junctions, instrumentation and the like. The reason was finally understood to be the dramatic effect of the very low air density at high altitude on compressor efficiency.

Another problem concerned the engine installation in the Canberra. The Avon engines were mounted ahead of the main spar, which was pierced to allow the jet pipes to pass through. The size of the hole in the spar could not be increased for obvious reasons, consequently the Olympus engines with their higher mass flow had to be restricted to 8,000 lb thrust at sea level. As the aircraft climbed, the throttles could be opened progressively, until finally limited by reaching the maximum permitted jet pipe temperature (JPT). Early engines did not have any form of jet pipe temperature limiter, so limits had to be observed manually.

Engine tests regularly took place at 60,000 feet, where the handling of the aeroplane began to get tricky, because the minimum safe flying speed and the maximum Mach Number began to converge. If the maximum Mach Number was exceeded, the Mach buffet that ensued could lead to loss of control, similarly if the airspeed fell below the minimum, the aircraft would stall, leading to loss of control. One pilot described flying the Canberra at 60,000 feet as a bit like riding a unicycle backwards whilst blindfolded.

Flights at 60,000 feet became so routine that early in 1953 it was realised that the existing world altitude record was being regularly exceeded by the Canberra. At that time the record stood at 59,446 feet, set by John Cunningham in a specially modified

Olympus-Canberra WD952 airborne over the south-west of England. The enlarged engine nacelles, necessary to accomodate the Olympus, can be seen clearly.

[*Rolls-Royce*]

de Havilland Vampire in 1948. To set an officially recognised new record under FAI regulations, the current one had to be exceeded by at least 3%.

The first task was to suitably modify the aircraft, which mainly entailed a major reduction in weight, as it was calculated that the aeroplane would climb an extra nine inches for every pound saved. So out went the observer and his seat, the pilots dinghy was discarded in favour of a balsa wood cushion and Wally Gibb even wore tennis shoes instead of flying boots. The bomb doors and their actuating mechanism were also taken off, and a lightweight fairing fitted.

A specially sealed recorder was fitted, equipped with two 35mm cameras, one cine and one still, to make the record of the required two altimeters. They were calibrated at the Royal Aircraft Establishment (RAE) Farnborough, oddly enough at a rate of climb of 3,000 feet per minute, so the aircraft could not exceed that value without invalidating the calibration.

One critical item in any altitude record attempt is fuel weight at maximum height. Measurements were made to establish the minimum fuel required for descent and landing, with one overshoot being provided for in case of emergency. The amount came to 90 gallons, but it required precise positioning of the aircraft to achieve a safe landing back at Filton. The weather was obviously an additional critical factor that had to be taken into account.

For the actual record attempt a triangular course was mapped out. After take-off on 4 May 1953 Gibb climbed at 3,000 feet per minute in a westerly direction to 50,000 feet, where he levelled off, turned to the south and burnt off fuel until the amount remaining reduced to the required 90 gallons plus enough for the ascent. The climb continued to 60,000 feet with the engine set to maximum continuous power, then the throttles were pushed forwards to achieve the maximum jet pipe temperatures, and the climb continued until the rate fell to zero.

The maximum altitude reached was more than 63,600 feet. At that point Gibb very gently closed the throttles, and the port engine surged with a loud bang and flamed out. A second later the starboard engine followed suit. With no cabin pressurisation Gibb had to inflate his pressure suit very quickly, and switch off all the electrics to conserve the battery. The Canberra had to be brought down very carefully but once below about 50,000 feet there were no further handling problems, and a quiet descent to 40,000 feet followed where the engines were relit. Both lit up at the first attempt as they always did. Indeed, good altitude relighting has always been a feature of the Olympus. The author, on occasion, achieved hot relights following surge and flameout at 56,000 feet during later Vulcan testing. The final FAI approved value of the corrected altitude reached was 63,668 feet.

The higher thrust and mass flow of the Olympus relative to the Avon caused some unexpected airframe problems, one of which was damage to the tailplane in the form of sprung rivets and consequent loose skinning. This necessitated a stock of three tailplanes, one fitted to the aircraft, one set as a spare and a third set undergoing repair at English Electric.

The standard of engine to be used in the successful record attempt was re-engineered for installation in the Vulcan, and it began trials in this form, designated Olympus 100, in the summer of 1952. Flight clearance was granted in January 1953 at a conservative initial rating of 9,250 lb and the second prototype flew with four Mark 100s in the following September.

Test bed running had rapidly accumulated; by the middle of 1953 nearly 4,500 hours had been achieved. In the same year Dr. Eric Warlow-Davies joined Bristol from Rolls-

OLYMPUS PERSONALITIES

15 MEN ON
TOP OF
THEIR
JOB!

KEY TO OLYMPUS PERSONALITIES

1. ROY LEONARD—Olympus Compressor Machinist.
2. LESLIE F. MAYER—Installation engineer.
3. GEORGE BECK—Olympus-Canberra Fitter.
4. NEVILLE HOOLE—Leading Tester.
5. GORDON LEWIS — Performance Technician.
6. DICK FOSTER—Olympus Design Office.
7. " DOUG " COLLETT—Test Superintendent.
8. BOB CHRISTMAS —Installation Engineer.
9. TOM PARKINSON—Chargehand, Fitting Shop.
10. PETER MURPHY — Stress Engineer.
11. PAUL HILLS—Project Engineer.
12. BENNY WOODROOFE — Coppersmith.
13. Mr. FREDDIE MAYER—Chief Installation Engineer.
14. Mr. JIM CUTTS —Chief Turbine Test Engineer.
15. " BRUIN " FALLA — Test Engineer.

A selection of 'Olympus personalities' - some of the engineers concerned with Olympus development in late 1952.   [*British Aerospace*]

Royce. Initially responsible for turbine development, he was subsequently appointed Deputy Chief Engineer in 1955.

Following the record flight, Olympus flight development settled back into a routine. The first production model, the Mark 101, produced 11,000 lb thrust at an overall pressure ratio of 10 to 1 and received its airworthiness Type Test certificate in December 1952. It was progressively developed into the B.01 11 of 12,000 lb thrust by the addition of a zero stage and uprating in which form it became the Mark 102.

During this time investigations were also carried out into the possibility of augmenting the thrust by the use of reheat, or afterburning. The injection of fuel into the jet pipe downstream of the turbines can greatly increase the thrust available, albeit at the expense of increased fuel consumption and usually more mechanical complexity, as a variable final nozzle is an essential part of any operational reheat system.

For initial investigations a system called the Bristol Simplified Reheat (BSR) was devised which was based upon the idea that a small but useful thrust boost could be obtained by restricting the reheat temperature to a moderate value. This would yield an increase in static thrust of about 15% to 20% without any significant increase in jet pipe diameter, and could thus be used in aircraft where the available space precluded a more complex system. The low reheat temperature of BSR could frequently be achieved by employing the excess capacity of the normal engine fuel pump without having recourse to a reheat fuel pump with a consequent weight saving. Some form of variable area final nozzle was required, so a simple two position device was evolved which weighed only 25 to 30 lb.

The initial bench research was carried out on a jet version of the Proteus, the lessons being incorporated into a system designed for the Olympus 100. During bench running with the Olympus a true thrust increase of 16% at a reheat efficiency of 85% was attained. The first flight test of BSR was carried out jointly by Bristol and the National Gas Turbine Establishment (NGTE) using a Derwent V mounted in a Lincoln, good results being obtained up to 30,000 feet. In Canada, Orenda Engines flew BSR on an Orenda up to 49,000 feet with satisfactory results. An Olympus 100 with BSR was flown in the Avro Ashton at Filton, and reheat combustion was satisfactory up to 40,000 feet, the ceiling of the aircraft. Reheat light-ups had also been achieved up to 35,000 feet using spark ignition.

An agreement was reached with the Solar Aircraft Company of San Diego, California, under which Solar undertook to assist Bristol Engines in all aspects of the design and development of full reheat, or afterburning, for Bristol Engines. In 1955 Solar proposed a design, and had manufactured bench units, for a full high temperature (1525°C) reheat system for the Olympus 101 and 102. Solar were developing a neat method of controlling the area of the jet pipe nozzle with a device known as a microjet, the purpose of which was to maintain a constant turbine pressure ratio, and as a result of the agreement, full details of the device were made known to Bristol.

An agreement was also concluded with the French aero-engine manufacturer Snecma about the same time, under which the Government-owned company placed the whole of their experience in thrust reverser development at the disposal of Bristol. Designs for Orpheus and Olympus engines were planned, an interesting precursor of a later, more fruitful, collaboration, and an early design of silencer was flight tested in the Canberra in the same year.

The basic 101 weighed only 3,650 lb, whereas the roughly comparable American J57 turned the scales at 4,200 lb. With the added attraction of reheat the Olympus offered to a number of aircraft designers the prospect of a relatively lightweight high thrust

Some of the ground crew who were associated with the Olympus-Canberra. From left-to-right, standing, they are:- Dave Preston, ?, 'Joe, the Lister driver', Bill Harding, Wally Haskins, Phil Meyler. Kneeling:- Ron Downes, George Beck, Ivor Type, Harry Grant. [Rolls-Royce]

27

turbojet for supersonic applications. The Bristol Aeroplane Company had begun investigations into a supersonic fighter in the late 1940s. Designated T180 it was to have been powered by two Bristol turbojets of 9,000 lb thrust, almost certainly Olympus. Unfortunately, like many such schemes of that era, it never progressed beyond the drawing board. One which did was a Gloster project.

A supersonic development of the Javelin, it was known as the thin-wing Javelin, and carried the Gloster designation of P370. It was initially powered by two 'handed' Olympus engines, 6/1 being the port installation, and 6/2 the starboard. It subsequently evolved into the P376 to British Government specification F153D, and with two B.01 21R engines of 28,500 lb thrust with 2,000°K reheat, would have attained Mach 1.82 at 36,000 feet. B.01 21 engines with the full reheat rating were promised for the P376 by September 1958, and an order for 18 prototypes was placed by the Ministry of Supply in late 1955; prior to that date Glosters had provided Bristol with a brand new Javelin F(AW) 1, serial number XA564. It was delivered to Filton on 14 October 1955, in order that early flight experience could be gained on B.01 6 engines in a representative airframe. Unfortunately one of the frequent changes in Government defence policy led to the project being cancelled in July 1956 before XA564 flew. Somehow the airframe survived the cancellation and it can still be seen at the Cosford Air and Space Museum.

It had been recognised quite early that the Canberra, although a superb test vehicle, lacked the internal space for truly comprehensive test instrumentation. Furthermore the engines fitted were prime movers and hence not only had to be of a very high standard but could have fewer liberties taken with them. In order to meet these criticisms a second aircraft was delivered to Filton to take part in the flight development programme.

Avro Ashton WB493 was delivered to the flight hangar on 8 May 1953, just four days after the Canberra captured the altitude record for the first time. The Avro Type 706 Ashton was basically a derivative of the Nene powered Tudor 8, but used a Tudor 2 airframe fitted with a tricycle undercarriage. It was powered by four Rolls-Royce Nene 5s mounted in pairs in underwing nacelles.

WB493 first flew on 18 December 1951 at Woodford, and was delivered to RAF Farnborough for high-altitude brush wear investigation and instrument development. It was subsequently refurbished at Woodford and then delivered to Filton.

The modifications necessary to enable the Olympus to be fitted were relatively simple, and were helped by the fact that Ashton employed what was virtually the original Lancaster wing. The pick-up points for the outboard Merlins were considered suitable anchorages for the simple Olympus nacelles, and these were consequently located below the wings outboard of the Nenes. Some structural strengthening was carried out, following consultation with A.V. Roe.

Although in themselves widely different aircraft, the test roles of the Ashton and Canberra were complementary. The Canberra had superior performance but could carry only a crew of two, had limited space for instrumentation and used the engines as prime movers. The Ashton possessed a more modest performance, being limited to about 0.6 Mach Number at 40,000 feet, but had ample room for comprehensive instrumentation and test systems such as water spray rigs for anti-icing clearance and in addition had adequate room for the crew necessary to operate them.

The first flight of the Ashton at Filton occurred on 8 February 1955 with Olympus 97s, and the first few flights were dedicated to assessing the aircraft handling with the centre of gravity at varying positions. Subsequent flights concentrated on developing an engine governor which combined the qualities of accuracy and stability. Governors

An Olympus Mark 6R (recognisable by the split compressor casing) running with reheat in operation on Number 104 test bed. The 6R had a maximum sea-level thrust of 21,680 pounds with reheat. [*Rolls-Royce*]

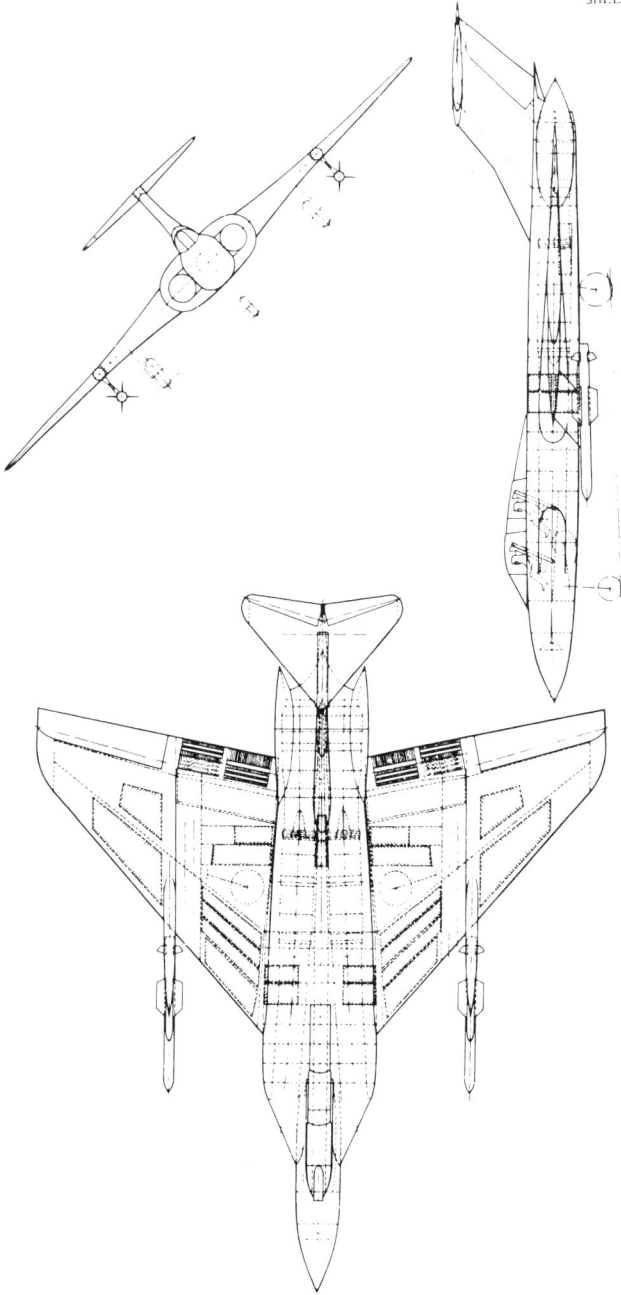

PROPOSED DEVELOPMENT OF GLOSTER F153D   P.376   ISSUE 2

The Gloster F153D was a supersonic development of the Gloster Javelin all-weather fighter, and it was to have been powered by two Olympus Mark 21R engines. The maximum Mach number was estimated to be 1.82 at 45,000 feet. [*Rolls-Royce*]

30

Avro Ashton WB493 painted (port side only) in the fictitious airline markings for the film 'Cone of Silence'. The water spray grid used for the de-icing tests is visible ahead of the starboard Olympus pod. [Rolls-Royce]

of the Standard Single and Double Datum types for maximum take-off and maximum cruise ratings were assessed.

Normally takeoffs were performed with all engines operating whilst landings were made with the test engines shut down. However, calculations had shown that directional control could not be maintained even with the use of full rudder if one Olympus failed with the other at full power at airspeeds of less than 150 knots. Accordingly they were restricted to 3,000 lb thrust for take off. Flight tests proceeded smoothly, however one early sortie on the 19 April 1955 was cut short when thick smoke from a defective air conditioning system filled the cabin.

The Olympus nacelles, being underneath the wings, had very little ground clearance. There was also a hazard to personnel, as one unwary member of the ground crew found out when he walked in front of an operating Olympus during a ground run and was sucked into the intake. Luckily for him the pilot saw the flicker of movement as he vanished into the intake, and chopped the throttle to shut off as the engine surged in protest. The fitter, Leo Flynn, survived with the loss of only a few fingers, and remained in the flight hangar until his retirement a few years ago.

By 1955 the thrust of the Olympus in its B.01 11 form had reached 12,000 lb, and certain engineers at Patchway were of the opinion that a reasonable chance existed of breaking the height record set in 1953. Wally Gibb was sceptical about this, but did not oppose the plan. In August of that year the weight reduction procedures were followed again, with a difference. On the second occasion the electric starter motors, which weighted 200 lb each, were removed, blanked and the cowlings closed after the engines had been started for the record attempt. To describe the flight itself, I can do no better than use Wally Gibb's own words, as published in the Rolls-Royce Magazine.

"The flight plan was almost identical to two years previously, although this time, having become much more accustomed to the aeroplane, we worked to a lower fuel reserve.

We took off on 29 August and climbed to 50,000 feet and, when the fuel had got down to the predetermined level, started the climb back towards Filton. Naturally I had clearly in my mind the figure which I had to see on the altimeter to ensure that I had created a new record.

With both engines on maximum continuous and their jet pipe temperatures absolutely on the limit, the aeroplane would climb no further and I had not reached the required altitude. It was obvious that I was not going to, so I throttled back a little and cruised for another ten minutes or so and then had another go. Again the altitude was a few hundred feet short of the record, so I eased the throttles forward a bit and exceeded the jet pipe temperature limits by 50°C. The aeroplane climbed the few hundred feet and I was certain I had beaten the record. I closed the throttles and descended.

The engines by now had much more development and did not go out, which left me with all the residual thrust from the high idle speed and the consequent descent problem. It took me 3 1/2 minutes to descend the first 10,000 feet, coming down as fast as the aircraft capabilities permitted. The descent through the other 55,000 feet was made in nine minutes.

After all the figures had been analysed, we found we had beaten our own record but only by overtemperaturing the engines, six of the (turbine) blades on one engine having been burnt in half. As a nice touch the Engineering Department at Bristol mounted one of the burnt blades and presented me with it. I still treasure it."

The final ratified altitude was 65,876 feet, just 278 feet more than the 3% increase required. At the peak of the climb, the airspeed had dropped to 122 knots, roughly 0.74 Mach Number.

The importance of the intake design and its effect upon the engine was not appreciated then as well as it is today. Nowadays permissible distortion and swirl levels at the engine face are precisely defined, even so we still get caught out occasionally whereas then the requirement was thought to be simply the provision of smooth air to the engine.

The intakes on the Canberra were simple pitot intakes, not at all like the shared intake on the Vulcan, and consequently a number of the problems met on the Canberra were unique to their installation. No attempt was made, or even thought necessary, to measure the distortion in the intake. Nor were any measurements made of the stress in the first rows of LP compressor blades. The technology of the time in any case was probably not up to the task. Be that as it may, the compressor blade failure that led to a complete haircut of the LP spool in WD952 on 12 March 1956 came as a complete surprise.

The Canberra, crewed by Bristol test pilot Paul Falconer and flight test observer Peter Little, took off from runway 28 at Filton. At about 50 feet altitude and 130 knots airspeed, just opposite the Brabazon hangar, there was a loud bang and the port engine failed. Falconer immediately had a serious problem because the aircraft was well below the single engine safety speed - with the Olympus fitted it was around 150 knots - and consequently the aircraft could not be kept straight with full power on the good engine.

To quote Pete Little: "The view from the back seat was not very good but I saw sky and various bits of the surrounding countryside pass by in rapid succession. We just managed to clear a cottage on the other side of Cribbs Causeway and made contact with the ground in the field behind. The aircraft jumped a hedge and we were stopped by a good old English oak tree at the far end of the next field, the impact tore off the port wing and fired the inertia switches. There was a loud bang as the panel behind the canopy was fired off and we were both out through the hole in less time than it takes to read about it.

The oak tree was good news as the next obstacles in line were a large pond and a group of inhabited ex-army huts - there were lots of surprised faces looking out. The helicopter picked us up and we were back in the office - Fedden House, currently the Product Assurance Department - within a few minutes of take off. The dead oak tree still stands just this side of the M5 but the pond and huts are long gone."

The crash rescue vehicles reached the wreck as quickly as they could, but not quickly enough to see the helicopter. I believe there was a bit of a panic initially as they searched for the 'missing' aircrew. There is also an unconfirmed report that the ground around the aircraft was covered in dead worms which had been driven to the surface and there killed by the spilled fuel.

Immediate steps were taken to obtain a replacement Canberra, WH713 being delivered to Filton on 2 January 1957. In the meantime the Ashton continued the task of Olympus flight trials in parallel with tests on the Orpheus, an early mark of which first flew in the Ashton in April 1956.

The development engines flown in the Ashton were Marks 97, 97a, 101, 102, and 104. The Olympus 97 for example tested an early mark of annular combustion chamber, which was being developed for the Olympus 200 and was fitted with sixteen burners. Annular combusters held the promise of a much smaller pressure drop than the cannular variety, unfortunately the early examples suffered from severe 'coking' between the burners.

Ashton test flying was mainly concerned with relighting, surge margin evaluation and general performance and system development, with particular emphasis upon anti-

English Electric Canberra WD952 after the port engine failed on take-off on 12 March 1956. The severed port wing can be seen in the right background, along with the tree responsible for its removal.   [Rolls-Royce]

WH713, the replacement Canberra. The flight hangar personnel are, left-to-right, George Beck, Dave Martin, Ron Downes and Leo Flynn. Leo survived being sucked into an Olympus mounted on the Ashton.

[Rolls-Royce]

icing trials. For this a spray grid was mounted ahead of the starboard Olympus, and water was sprayed into the intake at varying rates to simulate flight at different water droplet concentrations, with the engine at various power settings. The procedure was carried out at a number of different flight conditions when the air temperature was low enough for the water spray to freeze on impact. Cine film records were taken of the ice build up, the test being controlled by observers in the cabin.

In 1959 an unusual task befell the Ashton. A film was being made of David Beatty's novel 'Cone of Silence'. The plot dealt with a fictitious aircraft which suffered a number of mysterious accidents on entry into service. The makers of the film, Aubrey Baring Productions Limited, had asked Boeing for the use of a 707. The request was not only turned down, they were also threatened with a law suit if the aircraft finally used in the film bore any resemblance whatsoever to a 707. The Ashton was the perfect solution to their problem, as with Olympus pods fitted it was totally unlike any other airliner.

At that time the water spray grid was still mounted ahead of the starboard Olympus, so only the port side of the aircraft could be painted in the film's airline livery. This meant that in order to get the impression of aircraft flying across the screen in both directions some film sequences had to be shown in reverse, so the markings had to be reversible in order not to give the game away. The markings eventually used were painted in red, the layout being designed by Derrick Green of the Exhibitions Department. For the film, the Ashton was renamed Phoenix. The camera aircraft was an Airspeed Consul, so there were considerable problems in flying both aircraft in formation.

All the aircraft sequences were taken at Filton, the ground-running base alongside the main runway standing in for a number of exotic foreign locations, complete with potted palms. As a result, the running base is still known as Palm Beach. Virtually the entire flight test department stood in as extras, earning I believe, £5 a day each, which was not bad for those days.

Bristol had been aware of the Boeing intention to develop a jet airliner that was much larger than the DH Comet, and that Rolls-Royce had been having some success in interesting them in the Conway bypass engine as an alternative to the Pratt and Whitney jets. Accordingly a mission led by Dr Eric Warlow-Davies went to Seattle in 1956 to promote the Olympus, as it was thought that the absence of an overseas market could prejudice the continued development of the engine, which was then being funded for the thin-wing Javelin. No commitment was received from Boeing, and when the thin-wing Javelin was cancelled the very survival of Bristol Engines seemed to depend upon keeping the Olympus 200 in being.

Rolls-Royce also made a very strong bid to put the Conway into the Vulcan B2, to achieve commonality with the Victor B2 and to widen the home base for the sale of the engine to airlines in the Boeing 707 and the Douglas DC8. The Bristol team, led by SGH argued strongly for the retention of the Olympus, and their case was aided by the remarkable increases in thrust and reductions in specific fuel consumption that were made. Bristol's undertaking to complete the development using Company funds, and to peg the price to that of the fully-funded Conway was a bold and ultimately profitable gesture that contributed to the victory for Bristol and go-ahead for the engine in the Vulcan B2.

In the context of this argument it should be remembered that Air Marshal Sir Harry Broadhurst, Commander in Chief Bomber Command, had never wanted the Victor B2. He believed that his Command needed the interim Valiant and the advanced Vulcan and felt that 'the Victor was a waste of money.'

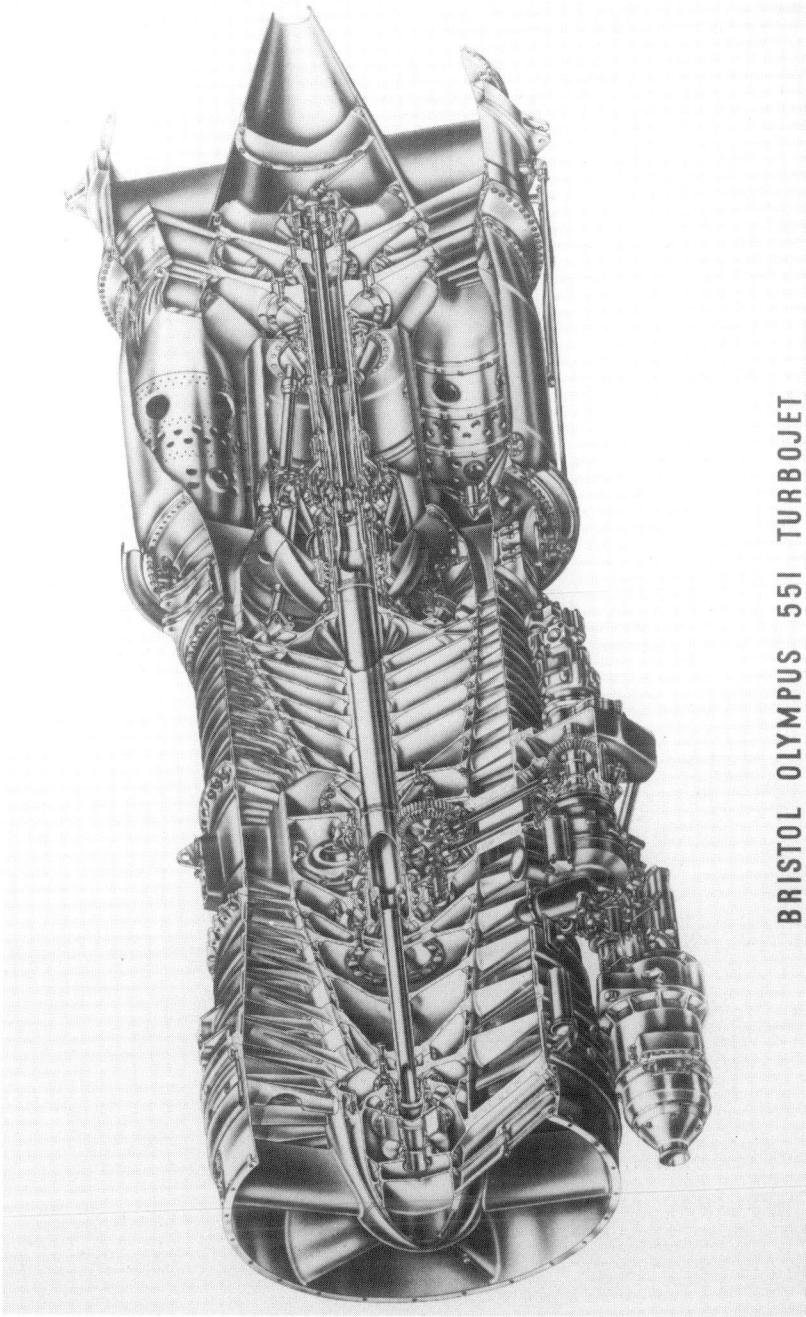

BRISTOL OLYMPUS 551 TURBOJET

A cutaway view of an Olympus 551. It was a lightened version of the Olympus Mark 6, derated to produce 13,500 pounds thrust at take-off. It was aimed at the Boeing 707 and Douglas DC-8 airliners, as well as being considered for the Bristol Type 200 and Avro Type 740 trijet projects.

[*Rolls-Royce*]

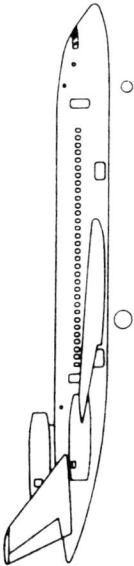

THE AVRO 740

POWERED BY THREE BRISTOL
OLYMPUS 551 S OR THREE
ROLLS-ROYCE RB141 S

SPAN	109 60FT
LENGTH	120 25 FT
HEIGHT	28 20 FT

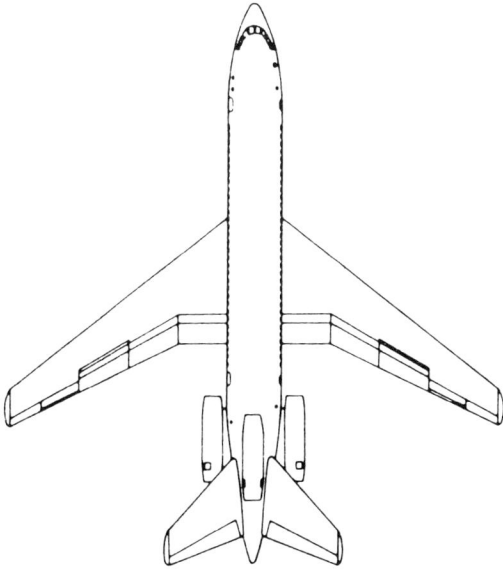

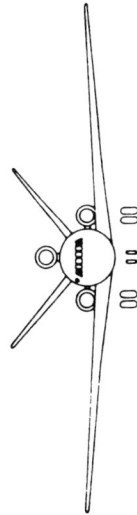

The Avro Type 740 trijet project. This was a contender for the British European Airways requirement that was eventually met by the de Havilland (later Hawker-Siddeley) Trident. [British Aerospace]

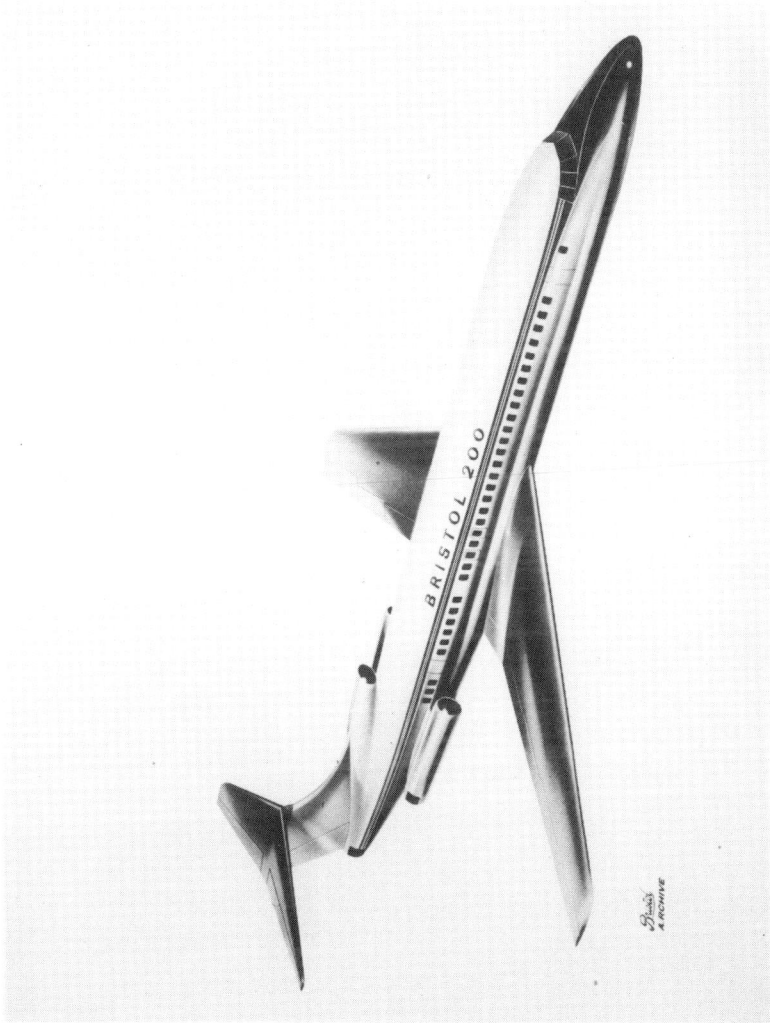

The Bristol Type 200 was designed to the same specification as the Avro 740. It was offered with either Bristol Olympus Mark 551 or Pratt and Whitney J-57 engines.

[*Bristol Archive*]

39

A number of civil aircraft designs considered variants of the Olympus. Early in the development of the Vulcan, a short-lived civil derivative of the bomber had been proposed named the Avro Atlantic. Intended to cross the Atlantic at 600 mph with 113 passengers, it would have been powered by four 'civilianised' B.01 1/2As. A more realistic design was the Avro 740, a trijet designed to the BEA specification that was eventually won by the DH Trident. The Type 740 was offered with three tail-mounted Olympus 551s or Rolls-Royce RB141s, the centre engine exhausting through the butterfly tail. An Avro press release said 'the Avro 740 will provide the last word in smooth, silent flight.' The Bristol submission was the Type 200, which started life with four Orpheus or BE-47 engines, but later was modified to a tail-mounted trijet layout with either Olympus 551s or J-57s.

The 551 was a derated and lightened version of the B.01 6 and was rated at 13,500 lb thrust at take off. At the time discussions were being held with Curtiss Wright with a view to manufacturing and marketing the engine in the USA, where it was to be known by the name of Zephyr; it was planned that a type test to FAA standards would be completed by the end of the year. A further development of the 551, the 553, was planned with identical performance but made still lighter by the substitution of titanium for steel wherever possible. For various reasons Curtiss Wright failed to successfully market the 551, and eventually the hopes that Bristol had entertained of selling an indigenous engine in the USA faded away. By that time the first Vulcan B2 had flown, and the Patchway factory was fully occupied in making the production 201. Development was also underway on more powerful versions for the Vulcan and other advanced aircraft.

2. Vulcan

Olympus Marks 101, 102, 104

In 1947 an Air Staff Requirement, B35/46, was raised which called for a high-altitude bomber able to carry a nuclear warload at speeds approaching Mach One, and to do so over very long ranges at a maximum all up weight (AUW) of not more than 100,000 lb.

The initial response of A.V. Roe and Company, who used the shortened form AVRO as their trade name, to the Air Staff requirement formed the start of project study number 698 by the firm. The Avro Type 698 began life as a swept-wing design, but soon evolved into a tailless aircraft, or flying wing.Further evolution produced the now familiar delta shape, but with small wing tip fins and rudders. In this form the fuselage had been almost completely absorbed into the wing, and the engines were mounted in pairs as close to the centre line as possible. However, it became apparent that the drag of such a design would be excessive at the design cruise Mach Number of about 0.9, so a redesign took place which introduced a centre fuselage with bomb stowage. This necessitated the engine nacelles being moved outboard, but still housed within the wing.

Concern about dynamic stability led to the introduction of a central fin, and the consequent deletion of the wing tip fins, because it made the task of attaching a tailplane relatively easy should one become necessary. About the same time the engine air intakes were changed from circular pitot entries to a more rectangular form which it was hoped would restore the intake efficiency to the original value. By September 1948 the layout was to all intents and purposes finalised.

VX777, the second prototype Vulcan, was the first to fly under Olympus-power. Four Olympus Mark 100s propelled the aircraft into the air from A V Roe's test airfield at Woodford, Cheshire.
[*Rolls-Royce*]

To aid in the flight development of the 698, a series of flying scale models, the Avro Type 707s, was built. They were not intended to play any part in powerplant development, but test flying did highlight a problem of longitudinal stability and trim variations with different power settings. As a result the jet nozzles on the Vulcan were angled to compensate for those effects.

The novel nature of the Vulcan led Avro's to embark upon a comprehensive programme of ground test rigs, one of which, the engine test rig, was unique at the time. It consisted of a port engine installation, with a half fuselage projecting forward some ten feet in front of the intake. The engine bays exactly duplicated the equipment and ventilation of the full size aircraft. The wing rig was decided upon in the light of experience that suggested that there were more difficulties in getting satisfactory running conditions with jet engines on the ground than in the air.

In particular the twin intakes were suspect since it was thought—correctly as it turned out—that disturbances from one engine could affect the intake conditions of the other. The rig was also useful in clearing the secondary cooling conditions in the engine bay for the generator and other accessories. Alterations to ducting and injectors were relatively easy to carry out on the rig and resulted in satisfactory conditions throughout with the minimum expenditure of cooling air.

Considerable engine running was carried out in the wing rig, more than 600 hours, which proved very useful in examining intake conditions and optimising fuel system calibrations for installation effects. It undoubtedly shortened the amount of ground running necessary when Olympus engines were installed in the second prototype, VX777.

VX777 made its first flight with Olympus 100 engines installed on 3 September 1953, at Avro's flight test airfield at Woodford, Cheshire. It was demonstrated at the SBAC Farnborough Air Show before being handed over to the Aeroplane and Armament Experimental Establishment—usually shortened to A & AEE—at RAF Boscombe Down, in Wiltshire, which is the centre for acceptance trials for all the military equipment intended for the RAF. Engine trials on this aircraft showed that the LP turbine stators had to be cut back to improve the engine handling, and this was confirmed by results obtained from the Olympus Canberra. This work was carried out during periods of aircraft maintenance so as not to delay the flight programme.

One of the engine problems experienced on VX777 was that of rpm creep at altitude, which meant that at maximum continuous power it was sometimes possible to exceed the maximum JPTs. The creep was greater than expected, which was partly accounted for by the effect of slight deformations of the aircraft structure in flight upon the very long linkage between the throttle levers and the engines. To cure this problem a cruise governor was introduced. The double datum governor incorporated a solenoid operated isolating valve to enable maximum rpm to be obtained at take off, the cruise governor being selected manually once the aircraft was airborne.

The Boscombe Down trials established the interesting but inexplicable fact that the worst engine handling was always found on the port inner installation. It was thought at the time that the nature of the airflow conditions in the intake was partly responsible. Little did they know.

During the trial the idling speed was optimised, and two other interesting problems surfaced. One concerned the development of the hot air anti-icing system for the nose bullet. The engine oil tank was located in the intake casing and normally achieved a degree of cooling from the passage of air. With the anti-icing system in operation not only was the cooling effect lost but some heating ensued, so the oil cooling arrangements had to be revised. Another problem concerned the pitot probe which measured the

The business end of four Olympus Mark 101s. The open engine bay doors and the drums on the floor suggest that engine runs are about to start following servicing. This aircraft was allocated to Number 230 Operational Conversion Unit at RAF Waddington.

[Rolls Royce]

total head pressure in the intake which was used in the fuel system to modify the fuel flow. The probe was mounted on one of the inlet guide vanes (IGVs). This tended to get iced up, so it was moved to a position within the nose bullet which had a large hole at its tip to allow the entry of generator cooling air. The nose bullet itself was heated by the circulation of hot air, and was sometimes referred to as 'the biggest heated pitot in the world.'

On the 27 July 1954 VX777 was damaged in a heavy landing at Farnborough, not through any fault of the engines. During the subsequent repair work Olympus 101 engines were fitted. However, this mark of engine first flew in the first production Vulcan B Mk 1, XA889, on 4 February 1955 following which it was held at Woodford as a C(A) Fleet machine. C(A) signifies that the aircraft belongs to the Controller (Aircraft), in other words the Ministry of Defence, and is used to indicate those aircraft that are retained for development leading to service clearance.

XA889 incorporated over 800 engineering changes compared with either prototype. VX777 subsequently flew with 101s about two weeks later. All these aircraft had straight leading edges to the wings. The 101s fitted to XA889 did not incorporate the turbine stator modification required for the 100, although it was equally applicable.

Meanwhile the development team at Patchway were pushing ahead with engine improvements, and were already talking of significantly higher thrust levels than those of the 101. When the Avro aerodynamicists heard of the projected thrust increases, they extended their calculations and predicted a high altitude buffet threshhold that could be almost reached in level flight by opening the throttles. Turning at full thrust would exceed it, and the resultant buffet would eat into the fatigue life of the wing as well as being uncomfortable for the crews.

In order to extend the buffet threshold, a new Phase 2 wing was designed, which had reduced sweep on the inboard section giving progressively greater chord to 78% semi-span, then a kink sharply increased the sweep to reduce chord to about its original value at the tip, the extra wing area forming a drooped extension to the leading edge.

The modified wing was flown in VX777 in October 1955, which then recommenced its flight test programme fitted with 101s. Following these successful trials, the Phase 2 wing was subsequently fitted to the first production B1 in February 1956 and the aircraft was delivered to A & AEE in March of that year for official C(A) release trials, following which the initial release was granted on 29 May. By this time a number of production B1s had flown with the straight leading edge, and these were all fitted with the extension as a retrospective modification.

Post C(A) release development flying on XA889 included the flight clearance of Mark 102 and 104 engines in addition to aircraft tasks. During this period VX777 was grounded for conversion to B Mk2 aerodynamic standard, and a number of other early B Mk1s were introduced into the Olympus development programme. One of these was XA891 which made a number of visits to Filton during its engine testing.

The RAF received its first 101-powered production B1, XA897, on 20 July 1956 when the aircraft went into service with 230 OCU at RAF Waddington. This aircraft became the first Olympus-powered Vulcan to be lost when it crashed at London Heathrow on 1 October 1956 during an approach in marginal weather conditions following a very successful tour of Australia. During the tour XA897 established a point-to-point record between Adelaide and Christchurch at an average speed of 634 mph. The engines behaved literally perfectly throughout, and the only attention that was given to them—two routine inspections—involved little more than the usual inspection and filter clean.

Olympus Mark 104 production line. The engines were built vertically in stands which allowed the engine to be swung horizontally when required.

[Rolls-Royce]

45

The 101 as received by the RAF was cleared for an overhaul life of 250 hours, and as a result of their usual very good condition when stripped, this was quickly increased to 300 hours, no intermediate flame tube inspections being required.

On 26 September 1957 three Vulcans left Waddington, flying non-stop to Goose Bay, Labrador and thence to Florida. The aircraft flown by the AOC-in-C Bomber Command, Air Chief Marshal Sir Harry Broadhurst, suffered not a single engine fault during the whole time the aircraft was away from the UK. During this period only three minor faults were reported on the other aircraft, including such things as a fractured pipe and a fuel control unit which permitted a slight rpm instability. Broadhurst's aircraft returned from Washington D.C. to Marham in 6 hours 12 minutes, an overall point-to-point speed of 582 mph for a distance of 3,645 statute miles.

The 101 was uprated to 12,000 lb and redesignated the 102, the main difference being the addition of a zero stage to the LP compressor to increase the mass flow. Trimmers were also fitted in the final nozzle, up to a maximum area of 6 square inches, to optimise the handling at altitude. The 102 was introduced to the RAF at a life of 200 hours and it was quickly raised to 250. By 1958, an unscheduled removal rate of one per 3000 flying hours had been achieved. An official report said, 'the Olympus 102 sets a standard of handling at altitude which has never been equalled by any other turbine engine.'

A study of the performance of the 102 showed that it was possible to take advantage of its potential by raising the turbine entry temperature, and that by suitable changes a gain of at least 1,000 lb thrust could be achieved. By careful attention to design the conversion was made applicable to all existing 102 engines and consequently they were all uprated to 104 standard, as the new engine was designated, on overhaul. This conversion involved the fitting of new turbine blades and discs, and burners of increased flow number to allow for the higher fuel flows.

The 104 was initially rated at 13,000 lb thrust at 6,500 LP rpm and 645 °C JPT, and it was type tested at that rating in December 1956. It flew for the first time in XA889 at Woodford in July 1957.

Initial tests of the 104 showed that severe rpm droop occurred in the climb. It was found that the air-fuel ratio control (AFRC) which was intended to operate only during engine acceleration when it limited fuel flow as a function of compressor delivery pressure was interfering during steady running and over-riding the speed governor. This was avoided by introducing a device which automatically isolated the AFRC at altitude. The idle speed at altitude was also found to be too low, and the full range flow control (FRFC) was consequently recalibrated.

The 104 incorporated the double datum speed governor and a double datum jet pipe temperature limiter. This enabled the pilot to slightly throttle the engines after take-off, select cruise rating and then advance the throttles fully without risk of exceeding the cruise JPT limits. In April the first 104 entered service in the Vulcan B Mk1 at a thrust of 13,500 lb.

Long range flights became quite normal for the Vulcan force, Lone Ranger and Western Ranger being two names applied to detachments to North America. A long range flight with a difference took place in late 1959 when a Vulcan B1 powered by Olympus 104 engines completed a round-the-world tour. The flight was made in order to take part in the opening ceremony of a new Airport at Wellington, New Zealand. During the return flight, a new coast-to-coast record of 2 hours 49 minutes was set on the Goose Bay, Labrador to RAF Scampton, Lincolnshire, leg, giving an average speed of 698 mph. During the tour the Vulcan covered 30,424 statute miles in 57 hours flying with no engine problems whatsoever.

A Vulcan Mark B1 being refuelled in flight by a Vickers Valiant tanker. This procedure was constantly practised when the V-force had a global nuclear role, but was discontinued when the Vulcans converted to iron bombs.

[*Rolls-Royce*]

On 21 June 1961 the Royal Air Force established a new world record for a flight between Britain and Australia when XH481, powered by Olympus 104 engines, completed a non-stop flight of 11,500 miles in 20 hours 3 minutes, an average speed of 575 mph. The Vulcan, captained by Squadron Leader Michael Beavis of 617 Squadron took off from Scampton in Lincolnshire and landed at Richmond near Sydney. During the flight the aircraft was refuelled three times by Valiants of 214 Squadron operating from Cyprus, Pakistan and Singapore.

Although at times the Vulcan reached altitudes of 60,000 feet the greater part of the flight was carried out at 40,000 feet. The fastest average speed achieved was 700 mph on the run across Australia. On landing at Richmond the crew of six were congratulated by Air Marshal Sir Kenneth Cross, AOC-in-C Bomber Command. Discussing the flight, Sqn. Ldr. Beavis said; "The Olympus engines performed magnificently throughout the flight and no adjustments or rectification work of any kind was required on arrival." XH481 returned to Scampton on 9 July after making a round trip of 28,000 miles in 53 flying hours.

In general the 100 series Olympus performed well in RAF service. Although a number of engine failures occurred in flight—HP turbine blades appeared to be a weak spot—only one aircraft was lost as a result, although several landings were made with one or more engines shut down. The standard Bomber Command drill was to shut down both engines on one side if one failed, because of the risk of debris being sucked into the good engine via the shared intake and thus rendering it untrustworthy.

On 16 July 1964 XA909 was flying near Anglesey when an engine exploded. The LP turbine disc was ejected, damaging the flying controls in the process, and as a result the aircraft became uncontrollable. The crew successfully abandoned the aircraft after directing it out to sea. It then perversely turned around on its own and headed back, finally to crash inland.

Subsequent examination of the wreckage showed that the sequence of failure began in Number 5 bearing when a fatigue failure of the Number 5 bearing cage adjacent to a spacer bar occurred. This resulted in a foul of the LP shaft in the HP shaft bore with consequent overheating, shear of the LP shaft and ejection of the LP turbine disc.

Olympus Modification 1316 had been prepared which introduced a bearing which had a positive oil feed to both cage rubbing faces, plus other features intended to reduce the likelihood of the LP turbine wheel being ejected. The modification was to be introduced during planned engine overhauls, but it was likely that a number of unmodified engines would be in service for a considerable time.

A test was carried out in an attempt to ascertain what, if any, advance warning of the failure could be obtained. An engine was run on the test bed, the temperature of the number 5 bearing drain oil being measured, and with the bearing cage already cut to ensure failure. This test showed that when the bearing failure commenced there was a sudden rise in oil drain temperature and that the ultimate failure occurred approximately one hour later.

This led to the suggestion of fitting temperature gauges in the cockpit for crew monitoring, whereupon it was pointed out that little was known about the variation of this parameter under service conditions. Accordingly a Vulcan was fitted with number 5 bearing scavenge oil temperature gauges, and a Bristol flight test observer flew on a number of different sorties to record the in-flight temperature variation.

A Special Flying Instruction (SFI/VULC/40) was issued which defined the procedure for recording the temperatures. This would only be possible on aircraft fitted with Vulcan Mod 1996 and its associated engine modification, which provided four gauges

The Patchway factory in the late seventies, looking north. Engine manufacture started on this site in 1920, in the three sheds on the left of the A38. The site of the Runway Garage is visible in the right foreground.

[Rolls-Royce Photo]

at the Air Engineer Officer's (AEO) station. The instruction was issued in September 1965, and few if any aircraft had been modified before the B1 fleet was withdrawn from service the following year.

Olympus Marks 201, 202

The increase in thrust that occurred as the 101 was developed into the 104 was gained by progressively increasing the mass flow and compressor pressure ratio by careful attention to blade design and by adding a zero stage to the LP compressor. It was already evident that considerable further potential existed in the basic engine, so work proceeded on a significantly uprated mark of Olympus in parallel with the first production examples. The new engine incorporated the results of much research into compressor and turbine blading and as a result offered greatly increased thrust without any appreciable increase in length or diameter.

The Olympus 200 started life with five LP compressor stages and seven HP compressor stages and produced 16,000 lb of thrust at a compression ratio of 10:1, passing 240 lb of air through the engine every second. It first ran on the test bed at Patchway in September 1954, under the designation B.01 6, but within a year a developed version known as the B.01 7 was producing 17,000 lb. In May 1958 the engine completed its type test at the latter rating and was then produced in quantity for the Vulcan B2.

The Olympus 200 could just be squeezed into the engine bay of a B1, and consequently four were installed in XA891 at Patchway in the Spring of 1958 so that intensive flight trials could be started. It was demonstrated at the SBAC show at Farnborough that year, and continued on Olympus 200 development both from Filton and Woodford until it was lost in an accident in 1959.

The Canberra accident, and other failures on test beds and in aircraft led to the realisation that the stresses in the compressor blades had to be measured under operational conditions. Strain gauges attached to critical parts of the selected blades provided an indication of the stress experienced under given engine conditions and these signals were recorded upon magnetic tape for detailed analysis. They were also frequently displayed in the aircraft on cathode ray oscilloscopes, so the signals could be monitored as the test proceeded. Although this technique did not permit detailed analysis, blade resonance in a number of different modes of vibration could be quickly recognised.

The first B2 was XH533, which flew on 19 August 1958. It was fitted with Olympus 200s and due to the need to get airborne quickly lacked many B2 features; it still possessed the old B1 tailcone, for example. The urgency felt by Avros to get a B2 airborne was indicated by the fact that the last production B1a, XH532, did not fly until February 1959.

Much of the basic work of strain gauge recording had been developed during the testing of piston engines, and the practice had grown up of allowing technical specialists to fly in aircraft to monitor their particular piece of equipment in addition to, and sometimes instead of, the flight test observer. This was particularly true of Mechanical Research Department, some of whose members would fly in test aircraft in order to monitor the blade vibrations.

This practice eventually stopped as far as military aircraft were concerned after the loss of XA891. This aircraft suffered a total electrical failure shortly after take-off from Woodford on 24 July 1959, and had to be abandoned by its crew, which included P.I. Christie of MRD. Phil Christie, now the Chairman of the Bristol Branch of the Rolls-Royce Heritage Trust, was the only Bristol observer on board, the task being a strain

A Vulcan Mark B1 ready for take-off. It was from this aircraft that Phil Christie, current chairman of the Bristol branch of the RRHT, made a successful parachute descent following a total electrical failure.   [*Rolls Royce*]

51

XH533 was the first Vulcan Mark B2. It first flew with 16,000 pound thrust Olympus Mark 200 engines. Note the lack of the extended rear fuselage fairing which was a characteristic of all subsequent Vulcans. [*Rolls-Royce*]

gauge survey at 50,000 feet. The strain gauge recording equipment was mounted on the cabin floor near the entrance door and Christie was out of his seat checking the recorder when suddenly the lights went out.

The Mark 1 Vulcan had an emergency battery which was supposed to give about twelve minutes of operation but frequently supplied less. As control of the aircraft would be lost when the battery failed, the aircraft captain, J.G. 'Jimmy' Harrison, knew that it was essential to allow the crew to escape before that happened, particularly as only the two pilots had ejection seats. It was not easy to get out of one's seat and squeeze past the next seat wearing parachute and dinghy pack and then step down to the entrance door which also doubled as an emergency exit, but fortunately for Christie he was already there. The complete crew made a successful escape.

In 1959 the second B2 XH534 appeared, equipped with Olympus 201 engines of 17,000 lb thrust. It was the first aircraft to have the extended rear fuselage fairing intended to house electronic counter measures (ECM) equipment. C(A) release for the B2 was obtained in May 1960, the first seven aircraft all contributing to the clearance testing at Boscombe Down at various times.

Olympus Mark 201s on the assembly line in Number 2 shop. The engines could be lowered into pits for easier access, as shown by the third from the left, which has been lowered as far as the combustion chambers. [*Rolls-Royce*]

Although XH533 was the first production B2 and first flew on 19 August 1958, the early B2s were used as trials aircraft, and it was not until 1 July 1960 that the B2 went into service with the RAF at 230 OCU. Ironically this first delivery, XH558, was to become the last airworthy Vulcan in the RAF, being used by the Vulcan Display Flight up to the 1990 season. All early B2s were powered by the Olympus 201, and despite the large amount of bench and wing rig running and flight testing, operational problems were not long in appearing.

The 201 appeared to be surge prone in service aircraft, surges followed by flameouts occurring on double engine handling at medium to high altitude. It was usually the inboard engine that surged first, but the pressure disturbance was immediately reflected into the outboard via the common intake. This occasionally resulted in the - temporary - loss of two engines on one side and although the relighting qualities of the Olympus were very good, the situation was clearly unacceptable to the RAF.

XH560, which had been delivered on 1 October 1960 was returned to Avro in November of the same year, having suffered several double engine surges, so that the problem could be investigated in a qualitative manner. A limited amount of instrumentation was fitted and flight testing started the following February.

After a careful analysis of the problem it was decided to cut back the LP turbine stators by 2% and that, coupled with a revised fuel system schedule gave surge free handling up to 52,000 feet over the required range of Mach Number. On the final flight a similar exercise was carried out with standard 201s, which surged and flamed out when slammed as a pair from flight idle. The test handling on the modified 201s included slamming from idle minus 2%. The whole exercise took over a year before XH560 was finally returned to the RAF.

The opportunity was taken to carry out other tests in conjunction with the handling trial. One such was measurement of throttle lever hysteresis. The throttle levers in the cockpit were connected to the engines by a series of linked metal rods. Consequently airframe flexing could affect the fuel flow and hence rpm at a given throttle lever position. The Vulcan airframe was fairly stiff and as a result throttle hysteresis was never a serious problem. It did however have the result that if all four engines were trimmed to the same rpm, the throttle lever quadrant 'looked like a bunch of bananas.'

Another problem examined was operation with the fuel booster pumps off. This requirement followed an incident that occurred on XH555 when it was on a production acceptance test flight with an Avro crew. XH555 had been carrying out some negative g tests at 40,000 feet when a battery contactor failed, resulting in the loss of the 24 volt DC supply, and all the fuel booster pumps consequently stopped. The engines began to run down, the two inboards flaming out. The tests that were in progress on the Rover auxiliary power unit required that alternators were selected off and hence the battery failure deprived the crew of the radios and intercomm as well as most of the flight instruments. The aircraft was in a difficult situation, above cloud and out of radio contact with the ground when a fortuitous break in the cloud cover appeared, at the bottom of which was RAF Finningley. A radioless approach and landing followed and an improved method of battery contactor attachment was swiftly devised.

The tests on XH560 consisted of measuring engine fuel inlet pressures with the low pressure fuel pumps both on and off. No flame outs were experienced even at 50,000 feet using Avtur as fuel, although it was suspected that had the condition been held for longer, a flame out would probably have resulted. The flame outs experienced on XH555, and on a single occasion in XL317 when the booster pumps had been deliberately selected off all occurred when using Avtag fuel, and could have been predicted had the requisite calculations been carried out.

A line-up of Vulcan B2s at RAF Waddington, in the original white anti-flash finish. The aircraft fourth from the top appears to be XH558, which is now used by the Vulcan Display Flight as the last airworthy example in the RAF. [*Rolls-Royce*]

One task which was attempted on XH560 is worth recounting here, even though it did not concern the engines. The objective was to assess the ability of the ram air turbine (RAT) to carry the full electrical load of the aircraft at 0.8 Mach Number and 40,000 feet. The RAT was a wind-driven generator which was hung on a bomb release in the port wing. When selected manually it was lowered into the airflow and generated electrical power.

The RAT was duly lowered and came on line at zero load as all four alternators were also on line. One by one the alternators were switched off. All went well, with the RAT picking up an increasing proportion of the load, until the last alternator was switched off. The cabin lights flickered briefly and went out, and simultaneously all electrical power was lost as the RAT tripped off line. There was no radio, no intercomm, no instruments other than the aneroids. Inside the aircraft it was as quiet as the grave. It probably took the Avro flight engineer, Bob Pogson, mere seconds to get two alternators back on line, but it certainly seemed longer. Needless to add, the test was not repeated.

The shape of the LP compressor surge line of the Olympus 200 series was very much like a wineglass, being close in to the steady running line at low rpm and opening up as rpm was increased towards maximum. In an attempt to match the overfuelling schedule to this shape without compromising altitude handling, the Lucas fuel system was fitted with a two position acceleration schedule consisting of a 'basic' line at high rpm and a lower 'split' line for low rpm. The changeover between the two was triggered by the movement of an opposed capsule stack, sensing overall compressor ratio, called the P1/P3 switch.

Early 201s had the P1 sensed in the engine bay, but a change in the basic running line caused by the 2% LP turbine stator cutback shortly after the engine was introduced into service required an intake vented P1/P3 switch.The amount of overfuelling supplied to the engine could be varied by recalibrating the acceleration schedule, which would move both basic and split lines up or down by an equal amount, or by blanking the P1 pipe so that the system only operated on the basic line. Engine surge could then be induced by progressively increasing the rate of throttle lever movement until the engine acceleration line crossed the surge boundary. For normal operation the fuel systems were set to avoid surge under all conditions even when the throttles were 'slam handled'.

The Vulcan engine installations were buried in the wing roots, each pair of engines receiving air from a common intake. The proximity of the inboard engine to the fuselage meant that under some conditions it could ingest the boundary layer off the forward fuselage, the inboard engine generally receiving 'dirtier' air than the outboard. The 2% cutback had been necessitated primarily by the reduced surge margin of engines installed in the inner positions. All engines had been so modified to maintain the flexibility of being able to install an engine in any position.

One of the more obvious characteristics of the first generation of jet engines was the smoke trail left behind the aircraft. This was denser in humid conditions and could be strikingly obvious if viewed against a bright background, a sunlit cloud layer, for example. The RAF was understandably very concerned about this, as it permitted visual acquisition of the aircraft very early. Even under conditions when the Vulcan itself could not be seen, the smoke trail pointed directly towards it.

In 1971 the first of a series of in-service trials was held to assess a means of reducing the smoke. At that time the USAF was heavily engaged in Vietnam, and was facing the same problem of aircraft being located because of their smoke trail. They had adopted the large scale use of a chemical additive known as CI-II. This very effectively

Vulcan Mark 2s on third-line servicing, probably at RAF Scampton, with two replacement Olympus Mark 201s ready for installation under the wing of a Number 83 Squadron aircraft. The further aircraft belongs to Number 27 Squadron.

[*Rolls-Royce*]

reduced the visible smoke in the exhaust, but had the serious disadvantage of being extremely toxic to humans.

The use of chemical anti-smoke additives was ruled out by the RAF and so a technical solution was required. The 200 series and 300 series were to be considered separately, with the former treated first. Bench tests revealed that there was a consistent relationship between the fuel injector spray cone angle and the density of the smoke emission, with the lowest cone angle coinciding with the worst level of emission at around 70% LP rpm. If the fuel spray cone angle could be controlled, a means of reducing the smoke emission was to hand.

The Duplex fuel injector fitted to the Olympus 200 series injected a primary fuel spray through a centre orifice. When the fuel pressure exceeded a certain value, fuel was supplied to a second orifice which was an annular opening concentric with the primary. Shroud air was blown through an outer concentric annulus to assist in the atomisation of the fuel spray. It was found that the cone angle of the fuel spray could be affected by changes in the size of the shroud annulus tip gap that the atomising air was blown through.

The first trial took place in an early Vulcan B2, XH558, at RAF Waddington. During that trial the smoke emission was effectively reduced, but Number 1 engine flamed out twice, and Number 2 ran at 25% rpm instead of 35-40%, following deceleration.

Following further bench tests of modified burners, a further trial occurred in March 1972. This time the aircraft selected was XL392, operating with 27 Squadron at RAF Scampton. Three flights were carried out so that smoke emission, engine handling and relighting could be assessed. Two sets of modified burners were provided and were fitted in the port engines.

The outcome of the second trial was that although the handling was improved, insufficient smoke reduction had occurred for the modification to be accepted. Undershoots below idle of up to 6% LP rpm occurred on slam deceleration, indicating that at least two combustion chambers were flaming out during the deceleration, although spontaneous cross lighting occurred after a few seconds at the sub-idle condition. Slam accelerations from sub-idle showed no change in characteristics as compared with slams from flight idle, but when initiated from the sub-idle condition took several seconds longer. A final trial on Olympus 202s achieved a satisfactory compromise between handling and smoke emission. The modification was accepted by the MoD and all 201/202 engines in service were so modified.

Olympus Mark 301

Before the 201 had entered service a proposal for a significant increase in thrust had already been made. The addition of a zero stage on the LP compressor allowed an increase in mass flow to 282 lb/second, and by introducing improved material for the HP turbine blades and liner the maximum thrust could be raised to 20,000 lb. Other changes included a shorter air intake casing, the fourth and fifth LP compressor stator blades were manufactured from steel instead of aluminium and the LP turbine throat area was increased. These changes were so designed that a Mark 201 could be easily converted to the new standard, which carried the type numberB.01 21.

The B.01 21 first ran on the test bed at Patchway in January 1959. Early notice was taken of the potential of this mark of Olympus by the Avro design team, who increased the capacity of the Vulcan B Mk2 air intakes to 700 lb/second at sea level. In order to gain early flight experience of the new engine, a Vulcan B Mk2, XH557, was allocated to BSEL. An attempt was made to deliver the aircraft to Filton Airfield on Friday 16

Vulcan B2 XH557 landing at Filton Airfield after a test flight. The port nacelles were converted to accept Olympus Mark 301s, with the starboard nacelles retaining the original Mark 201s.
[Rolls-Royce]

September 1960. The Vulcan made its approach late in the afternoon from the west in conditions of rain and low cloud and very poor visibility. It touched down more than half way along the runway, the braking parachute was streamed but failed to deploy, and with insufficient room left to stop in, the captain, Flt/Lt Wareham, slammed the throttles wide open to go around.

The Vulcan was at fairly light weight and so lifted off easily under the thrust of four Olympus Mark 201s, but not enough height had been gained for the tall lamp standards on the A38 to be avoided. Occupants of the BSEL office block were astonished to look out of their windows and see a huge white shape loom briefly out of the drizzle before roaring away, leaving the building, and occupants, shaking behind it. As it departed, the aircraft left a scene of absolute chaos behind it.

Situated alongside the A38, directly in line with the main runway centreline, the aptly named Runway Garage had taken the full force of the jet blast, all four petrol pumps being blown flat. A broken lamp standard lay across the road, steel railings had been torn down and two cars had had their windscreens shattered. The driver of one of them, Mr. Friedrick Gericke of Winterbourne, was doubly unfortunate. Just a year earlier, he had suffered a similar experience when the exhaust of a jet taking off from Gloster's Moreton Valance airfield had 'scorched the paint on his car.'

Tom Frost, BSEL Chief Test Pilot, who was in the right hand seat had clearly felt the impacts as the aircraft struck the lamps and not knowing the extent of the damage sustained by the Vulcan elected to divert to St. Mawgan, which was in clear weather. Before landing, the underside of the Vulcan was examined by the crew of a Boeing 707 which was also airborne in the vicinity. XH557 was flown to Filton on 4 October with the undercarriage locked down.

The B.01 21 was physically too big to fit in the engine bays in place of a 201, so a considerable amount of structural alteration was necessary to enlarge the bays. To minimise the time taken for this only the port inner bay was initially modified. Later the port outer was also enlarged, so the problems of twin engine handling through the common intake could be investigated.

XH557 first flew with a 21A installed on 19 May 1961, and was immediately despatched to Woodford for a two week handling assessment by an Avro crew. Engine tests with 21As and later 301s covered basic handling and calibration of engines, performance, strain gauging of the zero stage LP blades and relighting. The 'speed term' fuel system was first assessed in this aircraft.

During high altitude handling tests the engines would sometimes lock in surge and have to be shut down. Immediate hot relights were frequently achieved successfully up to 56,000 feet, albeit by 'milking' the HP cock. Whilst XH557 was at Patchway the V-force took on the task of low level attack, and extra flying was required to clear the 301 for the low role. This involved flying at speeds of up to 420 knots at 500 feet followed by a low altitude ballistic release manoeuvre. This simulated the ballistic release of a nuclear weapon, and consisted of a 2.5 g pull-up keeping the stick pull until the aircraft could be rolled out on the opposite heading. This testing showed that a resonant vibration existed on the zero stage blades within the running range at the higher airspeeds, and resulted in an immediate flight restriction being placed on 301 engined aircraft in service of not more than 250 knots below 10,000 feet. This caused severe embarrassment to the RAF in the training role. The cure involved resetting the IGV angle from -2° to +2° which increased the flutter margin at the expense of a slight loss of performance. Testing with the revised settings showed a significant improvement up to 400 knots at low level.

LOOKING ACROSS the Bristol-Gloucester road after a Vulcan bomber overshot the Filton aerodrome runway (in background), and took off again at the last moment. Blast from the jet engines and a trailing parachute used as a brake, toppled petrol pumps, snapped off a concrete lamp standard (seen near left), damaged the Runway Garage building and cars, and tore a gap through the heavy iron railings. Picture on right shows a close-up of the scattered petrol pumps.

The scene was one of confusion in the Runway Garage after XH557 overshot the Filton Runway in poor weather conditions. Petrol pumps were blown over, and a concrete lamp standard snapped off after being struck by the aircraft.

[Bristol Evening Post]

61

XH557 seen at high altitude whilst on a test flight from Filton Airfield. Such tests frequently involved prolonged cruising at 56,000 feet so that oil system behaviour could be studied.

[*Rolls-Royce*]

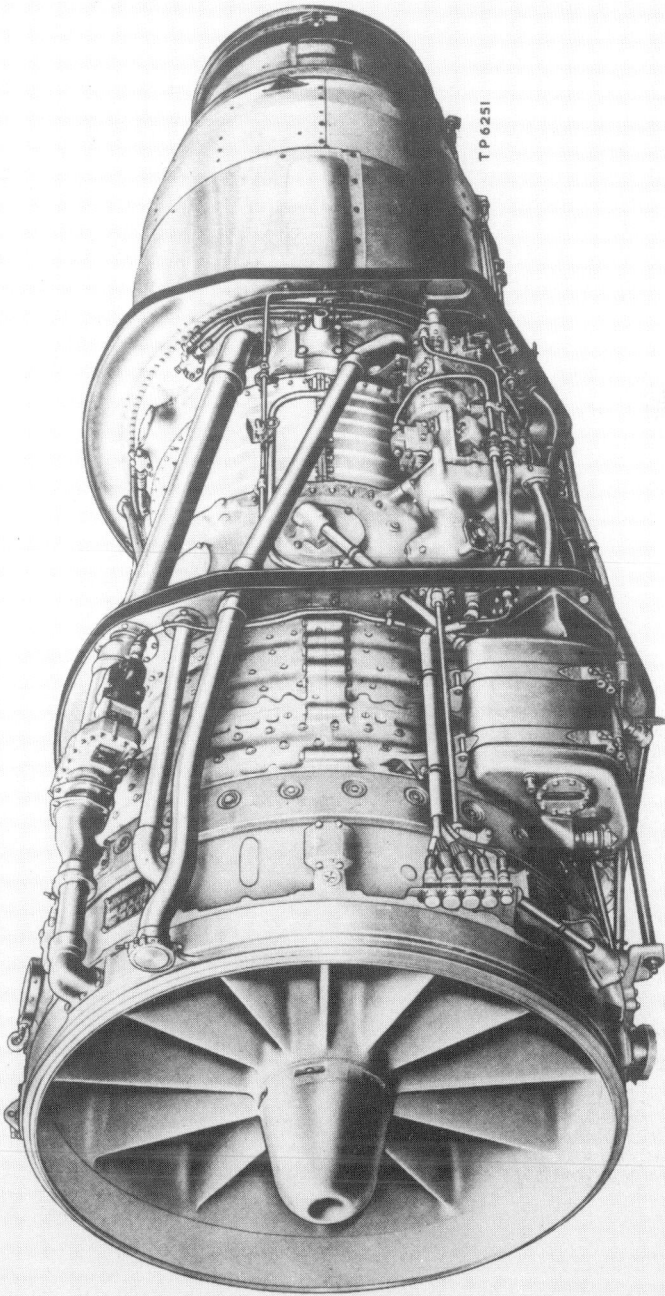

OLYMPUS 301 ENGINE – ¾ PORT VIEW

TP 6251

Handling on the 301 had shown a significantly smaller surge margin on the inboard engines. This had been apparent on the earlier marks of Olympus, but the increased mass flow of the 301 worsened the situation beyond tolerable limits, and the solution initially adopted was simply to raise the inboard idle speed by 10%. This was achieved by fitting solenoid-operated detents on the inner throttle levers which were automatically withdrawn below 20,000 feet and which could be overridden by the pilot if necessary. The presence of the detents caused some problems when flight refuelling. This usually took place at 30,000 feet between 250 and 330 knots, and the detents were switched out even though this meant that any handling had to be 'cautious'.

Later various modifications were tried to alleviate the inboard flow, such as varying patterns of vortex generators mounted on the inner wall of the inboard intake, and although a measurable improvement was achieved it was not considered significant.

The introduction of the speed term AFRC was an attempt to match the acceleration schedule to the surge boundary very closely. This initially appeared to resolve the inboard handling problem, but surge incidents led by inboard engines continued to occur, and the throttle detents were finally reintroduced, although at the lower figure of 5%.

Oil loss from the rear turbine bearing at high altitude was another problem that dogged the 301. Oil consumption rates of $3\frac{1}{2}$ pints per hour were recorded which put a severe restriction on the sortie length. Tests on XH557 involved extensive cruising at 56,000 feet 0.9 Mach Number. The oil loss was attributed to poor scavenging, but a quick fix which improved the situation was simply to drop the oil pressure from 80-85 psi to 60-65 psi. Ultimately an improved oil drainage was introduced which utilised an improved inlet to the Number 4 bearing drain pipe.

The Vulcan was an extremely manoeuverable aircraft, and consequently the engines had to tolerate treatment that one would not normally associate with bomber aircraft. I had an example of this treatment one day when we were returning to Filton at low level after a high-altitude engine handling flight. The aircraft was captained by test pilot John Cruse and I had the good fortune to be in the co-pilots seat. After checking around the sky to ensure that there was no conflicting traffic—no mean feat in a Vulcan—Cruse winked at me, and then gently eased the big delta into a beautifully executed barrel roll. Apart from a slight increase in g on the entry into the roll, he held 1g all the way around the first roll and then for good measure did another. It wasn't until the rear crew saw the Bristol Channel sliding past their high-set porthole that they realised they were upside down.

XH557 was returned to Woodford in 1964, to be refurbished and returned to the RAF. A total of 221 engine development flights had been completed, logging more than 300 flying hours.

In conjunction with the work on XH557, Avros had converted XJ784 to accept four 301s. This aircraft went to A & AEE in April 1962 for initial C(A) release trials. Following a limited clearance the 301 eventually entered RAF service in June 1963, when it had an initial premature removal rate of 7 per 1,000 flying hours. This subsequently fell below 1 per 1,000, then rose slightly.

Shortly after its introduction to the RAF a problem appeared that was to periodically recur throughout its service life. Reports of surge and flameout started to come in, usually affecting a single engine and not appearing to be biased towards any particular nacelle. The phenomenon was confined to altitudes above 40,000 feet, and usually occurred when the throttles were moved after a period at high Mach Number although there were instances of it happening as a result of aircraft manoeuvres. Post-flight

VULCAN B.MK.2 XJ 784   (B. OL. 301 ENGINES)

ENGINE INTAKE VORTEX GENERATORS

1(a) INWARD SWIRL (2ND. SERIES) V.G.'s

1(b) OUTWARD SWIRL   (3rd. SERIES) V.G.'s

These vortex generators were fitted to the air intakes of Vulcan Mark 2 XJ784 in an attempt to improve the inboard engine handling. A slight improvement was noted, but it was considered insufficient to justify fleet-wide use.   [*British Aerospace*] examination failed to yield any evidence, and quite often the engine would go on to complete many hours of trouble-free operation. Occasionally an engine appeared to be prone to the problem, and strip inspection and subsequent test bed investigation showed that these engines tended to the high end of the permissable range of HP compressor pressure ratios and that as a result there might have been a slight loss of HP surge margin. This however was never confirmed as the cause, and the incidents of random surge and flame out continued to occur until the Vulcans were withdrawn from service nearly twenty years later.

The spectacular nature of a Vulcan flying display inevitably produced many invitations to attend various ceremonies. In late 1965 two Vulcans from Cottesmore flew to New Zealand to take part in the opening of the New Zealand International Airport at Mangere, Auckland. Each aircraft carried a spare Olympus in the bomb bay, mounted on a special stand designed by BSEL's Design H (Tools and Packaging) Department. Neither spare was needed. Before departure, a vigorous test flight was carried out to ensure that the stand and contents would remain secure in flight.

The greater mass flow of the 301 raised several problems that had been of nuisance value only on the 201. Intake buffet with the inboard shut down and the adjacent engine at high power was very unpleasant and only became tolerable if power was restricted to 80%.

The 301 had a higher level of mechanical problems than previous marks. Four Vulcans were lost as a direct result of engine failure compared with one for the 201. The first loss occurred on 6 April 1967 when XL385 was preparing for take-off. As the engines were run to full power an HP turbine disc burst. The aircraft was totally destroyed in the fire that followed, but fortunately the crew, including an ATC cadet who was on board to obtain air experience, escaped safely. XL385 was carrying a Blue Steel missile which fortunately was a training round and did not have a warhead or propellant.

In less than a year a second 301 failed, ejecting the LP turbine disc. The Vulcan had returned to the circuit to burn off fuel following an inability to control the bomb bay temperature when there was a sudden explosion and a vibration that was so fierce the cockpit instruments could not be read. The Vulcan started to roll to port in an uncontrolled manner, pilot action to control the roll by use of trim and throttles being ineffective. The rear crew were ordered to abandon the aircraft but they had insufficient time to make their escape before it hit the ground. Indeed the captain delayed his ejection so late that had his parachute not snagged some high tension wires he would not have survived.

Combustion chamber outer casing failures led to the 301 being derated from 105% to 97% maximum LP speed, although this was restored to 100% in 1974. The final service rating for peacetime use was 18,000 lb thrust at 100% LP rpm and 625°C JPT.

Vulcans equipped with Olympus 301s were known as B2As. Rotax produced a compressed air starter for the 301 with which any engine could be started from any other engine by cross bleeding air tapped from the compressor, the first engine having been started by the Rover gas turbine unit. Starting all four together, a B2 could be rolling in two minutes and airborne in four. The Rotax air starter was retro-fitted to the 201, in which form it became the 202.

Olympus handling was generally excellent and this undoubtedly led some crews to take the response of the engine for granted. This happened with serious consequences to the crew of XM576 who were carrying out asymmetric roller landings at RAF Scampton on 25 May 1965. Following an approach with the port pair of engines

An Olympus 301 being prepared for shipment from Number 2 shop to the test bed for a production pass-off run.   [*Rolls-Royce*]

throttled to idle, all four were slammed to maximum for the overshoot. The 'hot' starboard pair responded more quickly than the 'cold' port engines that had been at idle for some time. The asymmetric power increase caused a swing to develop on the aircraft, which struck the ground with its port undercarriage which then collapsed. The nose wheel strut followed suit and the Vulcan swung off the runway, struck some out buildings, and came to rest in a car park with, as the technical report said 'considerable third party damage'. XM576 was later declared category 5, i.e. beyond economical repair, and was struck off charge later that year.

In August 1975 a smoke suppression trial was held on two Olympus 301s installed in XM648, operated by 44 Squadron at RAF Waddington. 301s with modified burners displayed similar characteristics to the 200 series, with the exception that the idle droop occurred after stable idle had been attained following slam deceleration, and did not then spontaneously recover. Accelerations from the drooped condition were smooth and surge-free but took 5-6 seconds longer than usual. The cost of the modification was estimated at £500 per burner (eight per engine) and £1,500 for the engineering to cure the droop. In the event, perhaps because of the short planned life remaining for the Vulcan, the 301 burner modification was not taken up by the Ministry of Defence.

Olympus engines with their greater potential thrust would have been used to power Vulcans equipped with Skybolt had that weapon gone ahead, and were used on Vulcans that carried the Blue Steel stand-off bomb, which itself was powered by a Bristol Siddeley liquid-fuelled rocket engine. Subsequently 301-engined Vulcans from the original Skybolt batch were used in the bombing and radar suppression roles in the Falklands War, whilst six 202-engined aircraft were converted to K.Mk 2 standard as single-point tankers.

301-engined Vulcan B2As represented the RAF at many overseas exercises where allied air forces tested their skills against one another. In December 1971 four Vulcans drawn from 27 and 101 Squadrons took part in the sixth annual Exercise Giant Voice. This was a bombing competition between the U.S. Strategic Air Command (SAC) and certain invited NATO air forces, and in 1971 coincided with the 25th Anniversary of the formation of SAC. The competition was divided into three parts, a night navigation exercise for three Vulcan B2As, 22 B52s and 2 FB-111s, a night navigation exercise flown by 30 KC-135as and a daylight bombing mission flown by 27 aircraft. This involved high altitude bomb releases over Greenville, Mississippi and Birmingham, Alabama followed by a low level mission over the Gulf of Mexico and terminating with four low level releases over Florida. One of the RAF Vulcan crews came fourth in this part of the contest; Vulcans regularly appeared 'in the frame' in these competitions.

One of the aircraft which took part in Giant Voice, XM600 was subsequently lost on a routine training sortie on 17 January 1977. A fire broke out in the bomb bay and spread to the port wing; the fire could not be brought under control, so the captain ordered the crew to abandon the aircraft. Everyone got out, with one crew member being injured on landing, and the aircraft crashed near Spilsby, 10 miles north east of Coningsby.

B2As of the Waddington Wing also took part in Red Flag exercises, where they were usually based at Nellis Air Force Base, Nevada. For these exercises they operated at night and at low level and achieved some good results, demonstrating that as late as 1977 the Vulcan still had the ability to penetrate advanced defensive systems.

Despite the obvious signs of strain in the 301 a further stretched version was projected. The Olympus 23 rated at 22,500 lbs thrust was to have been the power plant for the Vulcan B3 using the new Stage 6 wing. The B3 was planned to have the capability of

Vulcan Mark 2 XM595, in the markings of Number 617 Squadron, RAF, carrying a Blue Steel stand-off bomb semi-recessed into the bomb-bay. Both aircraft and weapon were propelled by Bristol products, the Vulcan by Olympus Mark 301s and Blue Steel by a Stentor liquid-fuelled rocket.

[Rolls-Royce]

carrying six Skybolt missiles or 38 one thousand pound bombs. The basic aircraft would have had a 5,000 nautical mile range, and had some of these been available in 1982 would have made a significant difference to the RAF's long range striking power.

In 1965 a requirement arose to re-engine the Martin RB-57F high-altitude reconnaissance aircraft. Concern over the increasing effectiveness of surface-to-air missiles led the USAF to examine ways of providing greater thrust in order to increase the operational altitude of the aircraft. Perhaps because of the successful high-altitude record flights of the Olympus - Canberra in 1953 and 1956, BSEL were asked to submit a proposal for installing two Olympus 301s in the RB-57F with the aim of achieving level cruise at 75,000 feet. Increased thrust was to be provided by uprating, increasing the turbine entry temperature by 40°C initially, and subsequently by a further 20°C. Hot end material changes were planned, so that an HP turbine life of at least 100 hours could be achieved on delivery. Concern was also expressed about the lack of 301 operating experience above 60,000 feet, so the test programme incorporated an initial phase in a high altitude test cell, where the ability of the engine to operate satisfactorily up to 75,000 feet was to be assessed. Any major problems encountered during this phase would have led to the project being terminated, however for various reasons the programme never proceeded beyond the study stage. The designation Olympus 701 had been allocated, the first mark number for an Olympus in the military export series.

The responsibility for the continued development and overhauling of the Olympus was moved to the Coventry works in the sixties, and the last engine to be overhauled was handed over to the RAF on 16 June 1981. The engine was the 759th to pass through the Ansty works in 17 years. The event was marked by the flypast of a Vulcan from RAF Waddington.

Olympus at War

In 1981 the long awaited run-down of the Vulcan force began with the disbanding of 230 OCU on 30 June at RAF Waddington. The first squadron to lose its Vulcans was 617, which converted to Panavia Tornado GR1s on 1 January 1982. The disposal of Vulcans began, the first one to go being XM653. However the increasing rate of withdrawal from service was abruptly halted when news broke that an Argentinian invasion of the Falkland Islands and South Georgia had occurred, a small Royal Marine detachment being overwhelmed in a few hours of fierce fighting.

Six Vulcans designated for possible bombing raids were drawn from 44 and 101 Squadrons, a number of essential changes being made to fit them for the task. Refuelling probes were refitted and crews trained in air-to-air refuelling (AAR) techniques which the V-force had not practised for 15 years. The bomb bays were refitted with conventional bombing equipment so that up to 21 one thousand pound bombs could be carried. Carousel inertial navigation systems were fitted so that the necessary standard of navigation could be achieved on the very long overwater legs involved in any possible bombing raids. The only engine change was the re-introduction of the original take-off rating, which would permit a maximum rpm of 103%, which was achieved by a change of JPT datum plug.

As flight times of the order of 16 hours were contemplated, a careful check of oil consumption was made on the transit flight to Ascension. The maximum oil consumption rate for the 301 was $1\frac{1}{2}$ pints per hour, which with an oil tank contents of $3\frac{7}{8}$ gallons gave a possible endurance of over 20 hours, but all the engines checked had rates of well under one pint per hour, so oil consumption was not a limiting factor.

The six airframes chosen were selected not only because they were 301-engined aircraft but because they were thought to have hardpoints in the wings capable of carrying external stores, a relic of the abortive Skybolt project. In the event one, XM654, was found not to be so equipped and it was not used. It should not be imagined that the locations of the hardpoints were well documented; in most cases engineering officers had to probe the undersides of the wings to find them.

The first AAR trials took place with Victor tankers of 57 Squadron less than a fortnight before the Vulcans deployed to Ascension, each Vulcan carrying an experienced Victor crew member to assist. Persistent problems were encountered with fuel leaks from the nose probes, with the fuel spillage getting on to the cockpit windows and completely obscuring the forward vision, not that the Vulcan had much to begin with.

In a local modification, gutters and vortex generators were mounted on the nose in an attempt to divert the spilled fuel. These additions horrified the resident B.Ae representative, who was convinced they would adversely affect aircraft handling. They didn't, but neither did they cure the problem, which was eventually solved with the assistance of Flight Refuelling Limited.

Air Staff studies had shown that a bombing raid in squadron strength would be necessary in order to achieve a sufficiently large number of hits on the Port Stanley runway to render it unuseable. The tanker force that was available to the RAF consisted of only 23 machines, some of which were on other essential duties. The number that could be allocated in support of bombing missions was only sufficient to get a single bomber to the target and back. From the outset therefore it was realised that the raids, which were referred to under the code name Operation Black Buck, would serve a purpose more political than military. By opening up the possibility of air raids on the Argentine mainland, it was felt political pressure would be brought to bear on the ruling Junta. A bonus was that fighter aircraft that might otherwise be used to attack the Harrier force were kept in Argentina for defence against possible air attack. In reality however, there never was any likelihood of permission being given.

On 30 April 1982 two Vulcans, XM598 captained by Squadron Leader R T Reeve as prime and XM607, captained by Flight Lieutenant M Withers as back up, took off from Wideawake Airfield in company with eleven Victor tankers. The runway edges were lined with piles of lava, and as a consequence the take off rating of 103% was not used in case an engine failure caused an uncontrollable swing. Shortly after take-off Squadron Leader Reeve reported that he could not seal one of the windows and that the aircraft could not be pressurised, so Flight Lieutenant Withers in XM607 took on the job. It is reported that when they heard the news there was a thoughtful silence, and then Withers said, 'Well, it looks like we've got a job of work to do, fellers.'

The eleven Victor tankers were there to ensure that, at a point some 100 miles north of the Falklands, one Victor would be in a position to give a maximum fuel transfer to the Vulcan, and still have enough fuel remaining to get back to Ascension. The Vulcan would then be able to carry out the attack and get back to a designated point south of Ascension for a final mid-air refuel. During the actual raid, a number of factors conspired to jeopardise this plan.

Due to lack of time no performance measurements had been taken on the Vulcans at the planned maximum sortie weight of 204,000 lbs and with external stores fitted. The Vulcans were fitted with a Westinghouse AN/ALQ-101 jammer, slung under the starboard wing on a 'home made' pylon that was attached to Skybolt hardpoints. The fuel burn actually achieved on the leg south was higher than expected, and consequently four 'prods' had to be made rather than the three planned.

Three Vulcan Mark 2s en-route from RAF Waddington to take part in the Falklands victory flypast. The nearest aircraft, XM597, carried out several anti-radar sorties over the Falklands. On returning from the final raid, a broken nose-probe forced a diversion to Rio de Janeiro.
[*Crown Copyright*]

There was considerable refuelling taking place amongst the tankers also, so that one would be fully topped up and in position for the final transfer. This did not go to plan either. The Victor designated to provide the last transfer was taking on its final fuel load in conditions of severe turbulence with the aircraft rising and falling through 20 feet when its nose probe was broken, and due to its own low fuel state had to immediately turn north. The one remaining Victor was not carrying maximum fuel, and could not therefore transfer the planned amount. Even so, the Victor captain, Squadron Leader Bob Tuxford, deliberately left himself short of fuel, knowing that he would have to make an unplanned rendezvous with another tanker if he was to get back to Ascension. To further compound the risk he and his crew were taking, he did not alert the staff at Wideawake to his desperate need for fuel until he was sure that the Vulcan was well clear of Port Stanley and on its way home.

After the last top-up, Withers in XM607 dropped down to 250 to 300 feet to stay below the Argentine radars, and all aircraft radios and radars were switched to standby. At 60 miles range the H2S was switched on for a land reference, the aircraft having to climb to 500 feet to get a return. At that height their passive warning receivers came alive with the noise of enemy radars.

XM607 then climbed steadily, reaching 8,000 feet with 25 miles to run. The run in to the target was made at 400 knots, and the stick of 21 one thousand pound bombs was released at 04.38 hours local time, the target being visible through thin cloud. The pilots could clearly see the flashes of the exploding bombs which had fallen diagonally across the runway, one landing on the centreline about one thousand feet from the threshhold. Because of the lack of opposition the Vulcan departed at high level to conserve fuel, instead of the planned low level exit.

The final AAR rendezvous was critical, as no assessment of the accuracy of the navaids on the Vulcan had been made after so long a flight, so a Nimrod was airborne to vector the two aircraft together. In the event the Vulcan's equipment proved accurate enough, and the Vulcan plugged into the Victor's hose to the accompaniment of sighs of relief from its crew. During the refuelling the Vulcan's windscreen became covered with fuel to such an extent that by the time the transfer was complete, only a small area about the size of a postcard remained clear. The pilots were guided in their formation flying by one of the navigators who stood on the flight deck access ladder and called corrections. Flight Lieutenant Withers and his crew finally landed at Wideawake after a 15¾ hour flight which was the longest bombing mission in aviation history. Throughout all this the Olympus engines had performed faultlessly.

Squadron Leader Tuxford had also made his much needed rendezvous with another tanker, and had landed before the Vulcan. For their achievements, both aircraft captains were awarded the Distinguished Flying Cross.

Some of the fuel consumption problems encountered on Black Buck 1 were due to the different cruising speeds of the two types of aircraft, the Vulcan flying at a higher cruising speed than desirable for maximum range in order to stay with the Victors. On later raids the Vulcan was despatched with an element of three tankers in support, with the main tanker force leaving later and flying higher and faster. A rendezvous was then made three or four hours into the mission.

A second bombing raid, using XM607 captained by Squadron Leader Reeve left Wideawake on the night of 3 May and bombed the Port Stanley runway after an uneventful flight. Due to a lateral aiming error none of the bombs struck the runway, although extensive damage was caused to the airfield facilities. One further bombing raid, Black Buck 7, was carried out on 12 June, its primary objective being the destruction of airfield targets, as by that date it was known that the Argentine surrender was not far away and that the runway would be needed for friendly forces.

The strength of the prevailing winds was carefully noted when planning the raids. This led to the cancellation of Black Buck 3, which had been planned for 16 May, when it was calculated that high head-winds would have reduced the fuel reserves to an unacceptably low level.

The Argentine forces had deployed several surveillance and gun laying radars on the island, including Westinghouse AN/TPS-43 surveillance, Contraves Skyguard and Fledermaus gun laying radars. The Westinghouse radar was primarily used to assist air strikes against the Task Force, whilst the gun laying radars were a constant source of harassment to the Harrier force. Plans had been made before the Vulcans left the UK to attack these installations, the Martel anti-radiation missile being selected.

Two trials with the Martel were carried out at the Aberporth missile firing range, and both were successful. However, before the missile could be deployed it was decided to use the Shrike AGM45 instead. As the latter had a smaller warhead it was felt that its use made civilian casualties less likely. XM597 was modified to carry four Shrikes, two on pylons under each wing and a short series of trials was carried out at Aberporth. One drawback to the Shrike was the need to set the seeker head to the frequency of the target radar prior to take-off, which tended to limit its operational flexibility.

The RAF crew who were to fly all the anti-radar sorties did not have an opportunity to exercise with the missile until they were on the transit flight from the UK to Ascension, when the AEO was able to track a few radars around Lands End. XM597 landed at Wideawake at 04.00 hours on 28 May, and Black Buck 4, the first anti-radar flight, was scheduled for the same day. In the event problems with the Victor tankers led to the raid being cancelled.

Black Buck 5 occurred on 30 May and was targetted against the Westinghouse surveillance radar, the Shrike sensors being set accordingly. As the Vulcan approached the target, the Shrike seeker head detected the appropriate emissions which abruptly ceased, although the gun laying radars continued to illuminate the aircraft. The Vulcan then orbited the Island for 40 minutes until the Westinghouse signature was again detected, whereupon two missiles were ripple launched against the target. The flashes of the exploding warheads were seen, and simultaneously the radar ceased operating. It was later discovered that the antenna had been destroyed, and the radar was out of action for 36 hours.

Black Buck 6 occurred on 2/3 June, and was aimed against both types of radar, the four Shrikes being set in pairs to detect the two distinct frequencies. While the aircraft was still 15 to 18 miles from the Falklands all the Argentine radars were switched off, and the Vulcan spent a frustrating 40 minutes trying to tempt them back on. Finally the aircraft was 'painted' with a Skyguard radar, the Shrikes locked on, and two missiles were fired. Again the flashes of the exploding missiles were seen with the radar simultaneously ceasing to transmit. After spending a further five minutes attempting to detect the Westinghouse radar, a low fuel state forced the Vulcan to depart.

The tanker rendezvous went to plan, but during the hook-up the Vulcan's nose probe was broken. With insufficient fuel to make Ascension, and no means of getting more, the crew were forced to divert to Rio de Janeiro. All the classified documents were jettisoned and an attempt was made to fire both remaining missiles. One however hung up, and could not be released.

The landing at Rio was made with the missile live, and there had been some risk that it could have locked on to a radar signal and launched itself, so as soon as the aircraft

Two Vulcans practising air-to-air refuelling (AAR) over the North Sea in 1982. The lead aircraft was delivered to the RAF in October 1960, and was returned to A V Roe in November the same year because of engine handling problems.
[*Crown Copyright*]

75

stopped, the AEO was despatched to make it safe. The Brazilian authorities held on to the aircraft for several days and confiscated the missile which was wrongly described as a Sidewinder, perhaps for political reasons. XM597 and crew were allowed to leave on 10 June, no further anti-radar raids being mounted.

The continued operation of the air bridge to the Falklands after the end of hostilities put a severe strain on the existing RAF Victor tanker force, which was not only inadequate to meet all the RAF's needs, but was accumulating operating hours at such a rate that its enforced retirement was being brought measurably closer. In an attempt to increase the number of tanker aircraft, a crash programme was initiated to convert Vulcans and Hercules to a single-point tanker configuration.

The six Vulcans chosen were all powered by Olympus 200 series engines, the airframes containing 301s being reserved for the strike missions. Three were from the initial batch of B2s that were delivered to the RAF, one of which, XH560, has already been encountered in this narrative. Vulcans converted to the tanker role were designated K2, and the unit that was to operate them was 50 Squadron.

To give an idea of the degree of urgency, the feasibility of the project was assessed on 1 May, an instruction to proceed was issued on 4 May 1982, and the first conversion, XH561, flew on 18 June. It was released to service on 23 June when XH561 was delivered to RAF Waddington. The airframes used were XH558, XH560, XH561, XJ825, XL445 and XM571. The last K2 was delivered to 50 Squadron on 27 October, after being evaluated by A & AEE Boscombe Down. All K2s had the capability of receiving fuel as well as supplying it.

June 1983 saw XM571 acting as a receiver during an air-to-air refuelling exercise at 25,000 feet over the North Sea when the probe broke off. A spray of fuel obscured the cabin windows and contact with the tanker was lost, so the captain initiated an emergency breakaway. As he closed the throttles all four Olympus engines flamed out due to massive fuel ingestion. Immediate hot relights were attempted and all four relit with, quote, 'The loudest God Almighty bang I have ever heard.' The number three engine was found subsequently to be damaged and was replaced.

Once the runway at Port Stanley airfield had been extended so that TriStar aircraft could land there, the demands on the tanker force fell rapidly. TriStars could make the flight from Ascension to the Falklands unrefuelled, so this released a number of Victors which returned to the UK. This in turn reduced the need to retain the Vulcan K2s of 50 Squadron, and by 1986 only one airworthy Vulcan, XH558, remained in RAF service. At the time of writing XH558 has very little airframe fatigue life left, and its future after 1990 is problematical. Some of those in private hands may become airworthy in the future; let us hope that the Vulcan will remain a spectacle at air shows for many years to come.

3. TSR2

In September 1957 a general operational requirement covering the proposed Canberra replacement was put out to industry by the Ministry of Supply (MoS) as GOR 339. The aircraft was to have a tactical strike and reconnaissance role, and became known by the abbreviation TSR2. At the same time Duncan Sandys in the Ministry of Supply (later to become the Ministry of Aviation) was intent on reshaping the aviation industry in the UK. On 16 September 1957 a meeting involving a number of aircraft manufacturers took place at the Ministry, at which it was clearly stated that the MoS would not place

Vulcan Mark K2 refuels a Tornado F3 fighter variant in flight.   [*British Aerospace*]

The last surviving Vulcan, XH558, overshoots the runway during an air display. This aircraft was expected to use up its airframe life during the 1990 season, and the presence of a Vulcan on the 1991 display circuit is very problematical.   [*Rolls-Royce*]

a contract with a single firm. Instead, two or more firms would have to merge together, so as to provide the industrial base that was thought to be required. The Ministry would prefer the firms to decide on the specifics for themselves, but was prepared to take the initiative if no suggestions were forthcoming.

A number of proposals were put to the Ministry by individual firms, and by July 1958 Vickers of Weybridge and English Electric of Warton were being pressed to get together. A wary exchange of information commenced later that year, and eventually, on 1 July 1960, the two firms officially merged into a new organisation called British Aircraft Corporation (BAC) with the express task of producing the TSR2. Also absorbed into BAC at the same time was Bristol Aircraft Company, already working on a supersonic transport.

BAC's first choice of engine was the Rolls-Royce Medway, which at that time was at a very early stage of development, whilst the Ministry preferred the Bristol Siddeley proposal of a reheated Olympus based upon a developed 301.

The engine manufacturers did not escape the so-called rationalisation process. In order to be given the contract to develop the engine for the TSR2, Bristol Aero Engines was obliged to merge with Armstrong Siddeley Motors of Coventry. The two firms had complementary, rather than competitive products, so the resultant organisation, Bristol Siddeley Engines Limited, (BSEL) possessed a strong and remarkably well-balanced range of products. The full merger of these two companies took effect from the beginning of April 1959, and thereafter certain departmental rationalisations occurred.

The basic performance of the TSR2 was not frozen until 1962. It included low level cruise at 0.9 Mach Number and low level dash at 1.1, about 725 knots, with a maximum of 2.05 Mach Number at altitude. The maximum altitude for normal operation was 56,000 feet and a clause in the engine specification noted that the engine should be capable of being developed to achieve satisfactory performance up to 70,000 feet. A radius of action of 1,000 nautical miles on internal fuel and 1,500 using external tanks was specified, and the initial rate of climb was estimated to be in excess of 50,000 feet per minute. It was to be powered by two Bristol Siddeley Olympus Mark 320 engines rated at 30,610 lb thrust with reheat at take-off. Thrust restoration using water injection was included in the specification, the minimum thrust in an ISA + 30°C climate being 24,500 lb. The Cumulus auxiliary power unit for the aircraft was also made by BSEL.

The development designation of the engine was B.01 22R, which indicated that it was a derivative of the B.01 21, and included reheat. The initial specification for the B.01 22R as defined in February 1959 was very severe, and went beyond existing experience in several areas, so it was decided to split the development programme into two stages. A derivation programme began in 1959 using a B.01 6 and two B.O1 22DR engines, the latter being essentially similar to the B.01 21 standard but with mechanical and aerodynamic changes to make them representative of the B.O1 22R. Much relevant information was derived from these engines in advance of the full 22R standard, including revision of LP and HP compressor blading, early tests of the 22R wide chord zero stage LP compressor blades and assessment of the main engine and reheat control systems, both electronic and hydromechanical.

The main 22R bench programme began in March 1961 and involved six engines, with an extra two being specified for a flying test bed. BSEL's first choice was an English Electric Lightning, a 400 hour flight programme being planned. Use of a Vulcan was discussed, the point being made that extra supersonic engine testing would be required in TSR2 if the Lightning was not available.

XA894 making a low pass over Filton Airfield. The bifurcated subsonic intake of the Olympus 22R can be seen clearly. The small projection under the tail was a periscope through which a cine film of the reheat flame was taken (without success).

[*Rolls-Royce*]

The material specification included a six-stage titanium LP compressor with an aluminium casing and a seven-stage HP compressor with four stages in titanium and the last three in Nimonic; the HP compressor casing was made of steel with provision for blade containment and both compressors were driven by single-stage turbines. An eight-chambered 'cannular' combustion system followed traditional Olympus practice. A reheat jet pipe incorporating fuel spray rings, flame stabilising gutters and a fully variable primary nozzle was attached to the rear flange of the engine by a bellows joint, the whole ensemble more than doubling the length of the basic engine.

The most interesting and forward-looking change was the introduction of an electronic control system which represented a very considerable advance over the electronic control fitted to the Proteus in the Bristol Britannia. It consisted of a single analogue control amplifier which incorporated an acceleration schedule with top temperature limiters and rpm governors for the variety of ratings and reheat and nozzle controls. In case of control failure a standby or reversionary control was provided which basically consisted of an inching switch which operated a DC motor on the throttle valve.

Reheat was controlled by pushing the throttle lever beyond the maximum dry gate and was fully variable over its range. The reheat fuel was injected into the jet pipe downstream of the LP turbine via three concentric spray rings, with three concentric gutters, or anvils which stabilised the flame, further downstream. The hot gas from the engine was not hot enough to ignite the reheat fuel, so 'hot streak' ignition was employed. This involved injecting a measured amount of fuel at three points, in the combustion chamber, downstream of the LP turbine and in the jet pipe in a carefully timed sequence so that a hot streak of burning fuel passed quickly through the turbine area and lit the reheat fuel.

The first bench run of a B.O1 22R occurred in March 1961, and although a number of mechanical problems surfaced during the initial running, a 24 hour flight clearance test had been completed by December. The most serious failure during this period concerned the combustion chamber.

In November a bench standard 320X (a 320 with a turbine of lower efficiency) suffered a flame tube failure that allowed hot gas to burn through the HP turbine bearing support and subsequently the LP drive shaft resulting in the ejection of the LP turbine disc, which did its best to demolish the test bed. It was thought to be an isolated case, and the preparations for the Vulcan were allowed to proceed unchanged. The flame tube was redesigned, no further failures occurring.

The test bed programme contained a significant amount of heated intake testing, an essential prerequisite for any engine designed to spend extended periods at supersonic conditions, and running behind a TSR2 intake. In addition operation at NGTE was intended to gain early experience of engine behaviour at supersonic conditions, and to provide confirmatory data for the flying test bed.

The aircraft allocated to BSEL as a flying test bed for the Olympus 22R was Vulcan B1 XA894, and it arrived in the flight hangar on 19 July 1960. It was to a very early standard and required over 150 aircraft modifications as well as being extensively altered to carry the reheated Olympus in a ventral nacelle. In order to simulate the length of the TSR2 intake duct, the intake design was simplified to be subsonic only, being bifurcated so as to pass either side of the nose leg. No attempt was made to simulate the half cone centrebodies of the TSR2 air intakes.

Ground running commenced in January 1962 with Olympus 22R serial number 2205. An important milestone in the contract stipulated that ground running must be completed by 31 January. Various delays ensured that the final flight clearance run

80

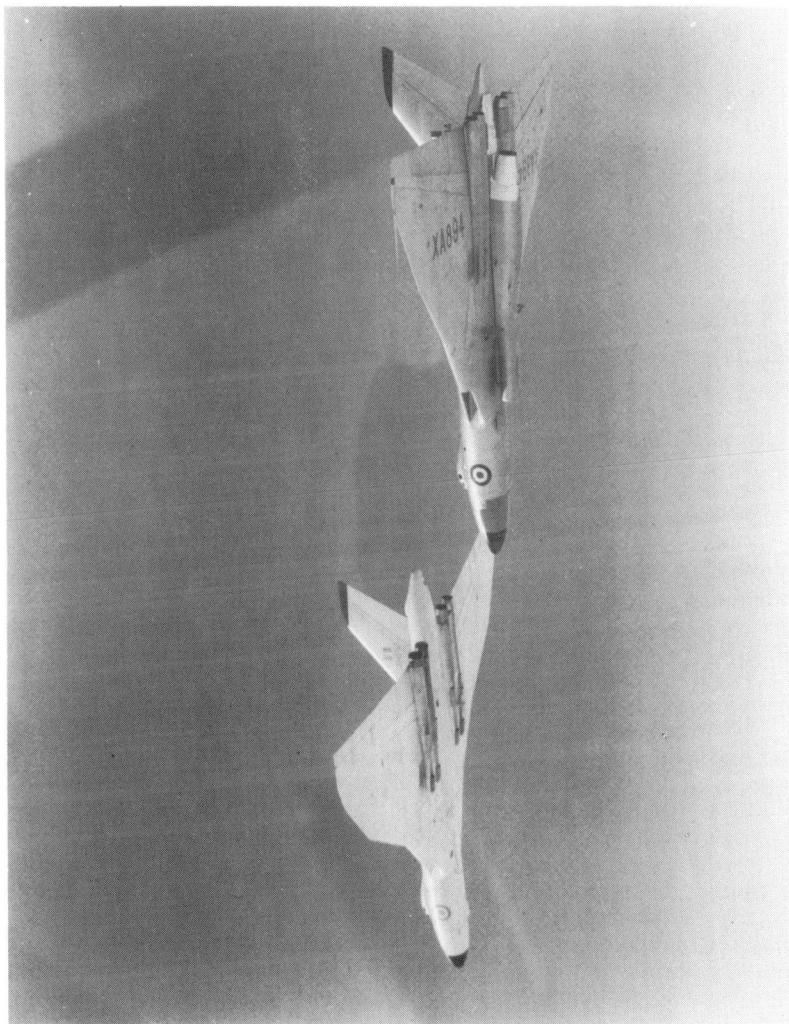

There are four marks of Olympus airborne in this picture. XH557 (in the lead) has two Mark 301s in the port nacelles (note the larger jet pipe nozzles) and two Mark 201s in the starboard; XA894 has Mark 101s in the usual places and a Mark 22R in the ventral nacelle.

[Rolls-Royce]

(Form 1090 clearance) did not start until late in the afternoon of the 31st, so in order to achieve the target, the run was continued until about 2 o'clock the next morning, much to the annoyance of the surrounding populace. The milestone was deemed to have been achieved because the run had started on the specified day.

The first flight occurred on 23 February, flights one and two being used to assess the handling of the aircraft with the nacelle fitted. The basic weight of the airframe had increased by about 20,000 lb, but the only operational difference was that approaches were made slightly faster, and no aerodynamic braking was used on landing, the braking parachute being streamed every time. The initial flights were chased by Canberra B2 WK141, and once the flying qualities of the Vulcan with the test nacelle were understood the practice was discontinued. Engine flight trials then proceeded with only minor snags until June, when the aircraft was briefly grounded to enable the engine to be rebuilt to the more powerful 22R-1 standard.

In May another 320X failed on test, the LP turbine disc bursting and ejecting the fragments. The failure had started with the loss of cooling air to the turbine disc, leading to failure of the rim and subsequent disc rupture. The sequence of events was understood, and could be detected before disc failure by close monitoring of the turbine disc rim cooling air temperatures, which were displayed in the Vulcan cockpit. No doubt those gauges were studied with even greater care on subsequent flights.

The aircraft was demonstrated at the SBAC show at Farnborough in September, the low level flypasts with reheat alight being particularly spectacular. Flight tests continued after the show, full three ring reheat being flown for the first time on flight 48 on 12 November. Wing Commander R P Beamont, the Chief Test Pilot of BAC Warton, flew in the aircraft on 20 November to assess engine and reheat handling. It was to be XA894's last flight.

During the afternoon of 3rd December, XA894 was positioned on the detuner for a ground run which included a full power check. At about three o'clock power was increased to maximum reheat, the exhaust flame very evident in the grey winter light with evenly spaced shock diamonds clearly visible along its length. Seconds later there was a burst of orange flame above and below the aircraft, which visibly lurched forwards. Inside the cabin the four occupants clearly felt the shock as the engine failed. Simultaneously the bomb bay fire warning lights flashed on and went out again, presumably because the firewire had been destroyed. The crew rapidly evacuated the aircraft, one flight test observer pausing just long enough to note that the LP turbine disc rim cooling air temperature was still within limits. The exit was not helped by the presence of the crew ladder on the door, it being common practice then to leave it in place for ground runs.

Within seconds of the crew escaping, burning fuel had poured underneath the crew door and engulfed the attendant fire engine. This had been in position, as always, throughout the ground run and its crew leapt into action with commendable speed. The fire was beyond control however and when the firemen saw that their appliance was ablaze, they turned and attempted to extinguish it. In the event, both the Vulcan and the fire engine were allowed to burn out. Throughout that long afternoon, as the aircraft burned, brilliant white balls of burning magnesium alloy rose in a continuous fountain above the fire.

Impact marks found on the ground when the debris was cleared away permitted a reconstruction of the sequence of events. The LP turbine disc had been ejected from the engine. The disc had apparently travelled around the strengthened bomb bay structure, carving open two 150 gallon stainless steel fuel tanks as it did so. It then hit

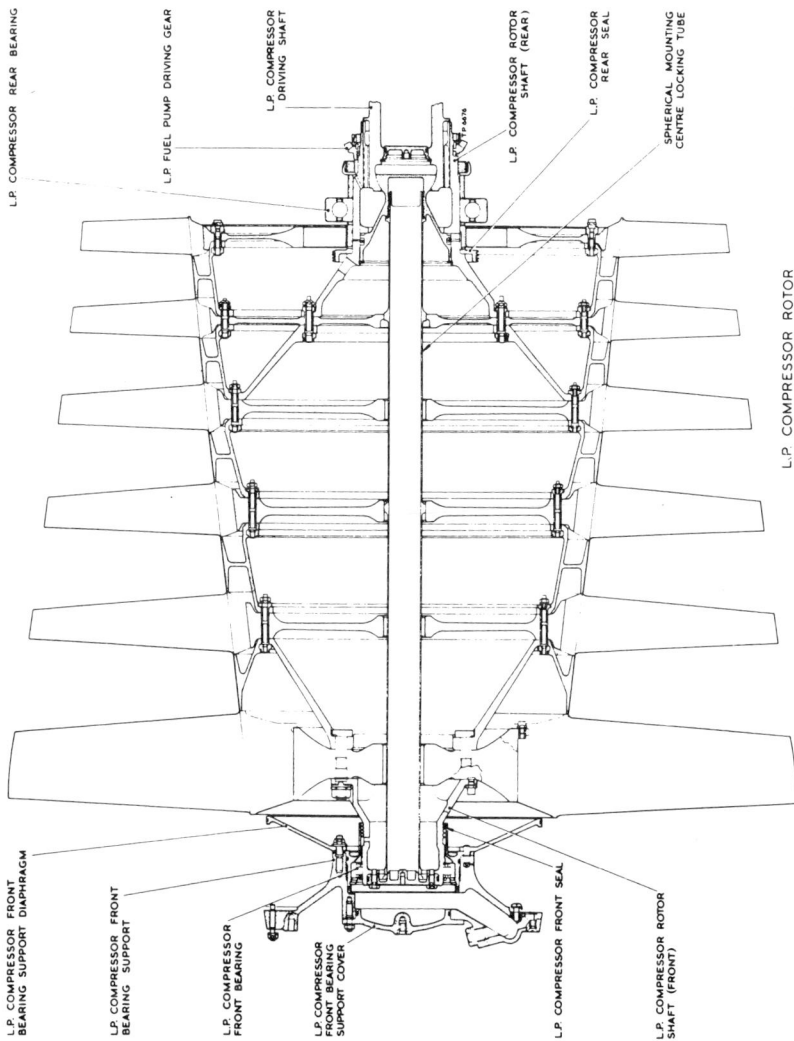

LP COMPRESSOR REAR BEARING

LP FUEL PUMP DRIVING GEAR

LP COMPRESSOR DRIVING SHAFT

LP COMPRESSOR ROTOR SHAFT (REAR)

LP COMPRESSOR REAR SEAL

SPHERICAL MOUNTING CENTRE LOCKING TUBE

LP COMPRESSOR ROTOR

LP COMPRESSOR FRONT BEARING SUPPORT DIAPHRAGM

LP COMPRESSOR FRONT BEARING SUPPORT

LP COMPRESSOR FRONT BEARING

LP COMPRESSOR FRONT BEARING SUPPORT COVER

LP COMPRESSOR FRONT SEAL

LP COMPRESSOR ROTOR SHAFT (FRONT)

This drawing of the low-pressure compressor of the Olympus Mark 320 shows the wide chord first-stage blades which were designed to withstand bird impacts at high airspeeds.

[Rolls-Royce]

83

An Olympus Mark 22DR, with reheat jet pipe attached, on the test bed at Patchway. The 22DR was an Olympus Mark 301 modified to be mechanically and aerodynamically similar to the Olympus Mark 22R. [*Rolls-Royce*]

The Olympus Mark 22R flying test bed with reheat in operation. The airbrakes were extended to reduce the acceleration of the Vulcan. Even with all four Olympus 101s at idle, it was impossible to keep a constant airspeed with the 22R at maximum reheat, so performance points were measured with the aircraft climbing.

[*Rolls-Royce*]

the ground, and presumably at that point shed what remained of the turbine blades, which must have sprayed like shrapnel into the starboard wing, rupturing every fuel tank. Having bounced off the ground it set off in an easterly direction, cutting a ten foot rip in the port wing leading edge as it went. The marks of its passage were clearly to be seen, savage slashes in the earth every 150 feet or so. It finally stopped not too far from the Bristol T188 which was being prepared for a test flight on the eastern turning circle.

The weather next morning was dank and foggy, and along with several other people I had the unpleasant job of sifting through the sodden aluminium ash that was all that remained, to find the missing turbine blades. Several things are still sharp in my mind. Some neat rows of small round cans turned out to be the remains of the cockpit instruments; the survival handbooks in the dinghy packs were still legible; a flight test observer's stop watch was still recognisable, although it no longer worked.

Careful analysis of the remains of the engine revealed that the LP compressor drive shaft had failed because of axial fatigue cracks through oil drain holes in the stiffening bands on the centre section of the shaft. This had resulted in a further failure at the LP turbine bearing and consequent ejection of the LP turbine disc. What was not immediately obvious was the mechanism that could cause the shaft to vibrate in the failure mode, and considerable effort was invested in the search for the cause and the cure.

Another problem that achieved a certain notoriety was that of HP turbine blade failures. The blades were initially cast in G64 material, and several engines suffered complete cropping of all the HP turbine blades. During the first type test to the 320X rating, engine 2201 had a failure which caused such severe damage that the combustion chamber outer casing split wide open, ejecting not only the HP turbine blades, but the flame tubes as well. After that a decision was taken to forge the blades out of Nimonic 115 which offered much better containment capability. The decision was supported by a subsequent blade failure in an engine which had a number of Nimonic blades fitted. The G64 blades suffered the usual cropping but those in Nimonic were still attached to the disc, although heavily damaged. A subsequent attempt to complete the type test again using G64 blades resulted in another complete cropping of the HP turbine, and combustion chamber outer casing failure although the containment shield remained intact. In order to prevent the problem carrying over to the 320, the containment shields were dispensed with and the turbine casing was thickened to provide integral containment, in addition to the change of blade material, and no further serious blade failures occurred.

Following the loss of XA894, Olympus 320 development at NGTE Pyestock was stepped up. Moves had been made to replace the flying test bed which had got as far as identifying a Vulcan, XA889, but the delay and extra cost proved in the end to be too much, so instead high priority was accorded to the Pyestock testing. Most of the running was carried out in Cell 3, which was a supersonic tunnel with Mach 2 capability. It had a number of drawbacks, however, the worst of which was the fact that it was a connected jet facility, that is to say the air from the plant compressor was ducted directly into the engine via a flow straightener section. Bias gauzes could be inserted in front of the engine face to produce various levels of distortion in order to simulate the effects of the TSR2 air intake.

The air supply system at Pyestock had a number of shut-off valves which were designed to isolate various sections in the event of problems. These valves were a little too sensitive for anyone's peace of mind, because they sometimes closed when the

XA894 burns at the 'Palm Beach' ground run site on 3 December 1962. The underslung Olympus Mark 22R had failed, ejecting the low-pressure turbine disc which then cut open the bomb bay fuel tanks. The fire engine seen on the left of the picture was also destroyed. [*Rolls-Royce*]

engine was running. Considerable development was required to get the valves to react correctly, and as they were up to 6 feet in diameter and weighed about half a ton each, it was only possible to test the operation with a 'real' engine in the cell.

In the centre of the Cell 3 control room was a large power consumption meter, calibrated in megawatts. The scale went up to 150 or thereabouts. The power consumption was so enormous that the plant was only able to operate at off-peak periods unless special permission had been given from on high. This was seldom granted so most running went on late at night. It was not uncommon to see a reading of 100 megawatts standing load during cell operation.

A more serious shortcoming of Cell 3 was its inability to react quickly to rapid changes in mass flow. The Olympus 320 could increase its mass flow from 20 lb/sec. to 290 lb/sec. in less than 10 seconds and during this time the intake pressure would fall significantly as the engine demand momentarily exceeded the capacity of the test plant. It had the effect of carrying out engine handling in a rapid climb, followed by an equally rapid descent once engine conditions had stabilised. As the jet pipe conditions did not vary in the same manner, the overall result was a little unreal. For tests that did not require a large change in mass flow, such as steady state performance or relighting, the cell results were perfectly valid.

In addition to Cell 3, a significant amount of engine running was carried out in Cell 2. Similar to Cell 3, it was designed to run at higher ram pressures and could thus simulate operation at high speeds in low level flight. Such speeds usually involved the use of reheat, and generated fuel flows that seemed unbelievable.

During the winter of 1963/64 the Canadian Research Council made available facilities for carrying out icing trials at their Montreal Road Laboratories, Ottawa, under the sponsorship of the Ministry of Aviation. The first engine tested was B.O1 22R Number 2205, which in an earlier build was flown in the Vulcan FTB. For the trial six of the eight combustion chambers were fitted with glow plugs, following 301 experience, and a short slave jet pipe was used in place of the standard reheat unit. The tests were very successful and permitted a limited flight clearance in icing conditions to be defined.

The main sub-assemblies for the first prototype, XR219, were delivered to A & AEE Boscombe Down on large lorries on 4 March 1964, final assembly being carried out in a hangar in the B Squadron area. As the date for ground running drew closer, a veritable army of engineers from BSEL, English Electric and Vickers, as well as from many of the equipment suppliers, descended upon the airfield. An office block was taken over for trace recorder film analysis, meetings and so on, and a ground running area on the far side of the airfield was fitted with the appropriate tethering gear capable of restraining the aircraft when both engines were producing maximum thrust. The running base was oval in shape and it became known as the peardrop to all who attended the TSR2 throughout the summer of 1964.

The peardrop was close to the airfield boundary that paralleled the Salisbury Road, and later when first flight was approaching it was quite normal to see lines of stationary vehicles occupied by the world's press apparently waiting for a scoop. At one point a small marquee was erected, and hot meals were brought across from the canteen so that testing could proceed without a break. I seem to recall that those 'hot' meals were usually cold.

Flight Test Department was called upon to provide the rear seat occupant for most of the ground running. His duties included keeping a detailed log and operating the instrumentation, the tests being controlled by BAC personnel in a nearby caravan. In the event of a serious problem, such as a fire, the very heavy partially-glazed canopy

The jet pipe of an Olympus Mark 320. The nozzle petals, visible inside the nozzle, were forced against the tapered part of the shroud by the pressure of the exhaust gas. Pneumatic jacks, visible at the left, moved the nozzle shroud fore and aft, thus varying the nozzle area.
[Rolls-Royce]

was to be opened manually, and escape effected using a long rope which was anchored in the cockpit. It cannot be said that the ground runs proceeded without problems. Not all these were of BSEL's making, but some were sufficiently serious to cause lengthy delays.

The first attempted dry cycle on the port engine only produced half the expected engine speed, but it was noticed that both engines were turning over. It was subsequently found that a cross bleed valve had failed open, and once that was corrected normal dry cycle speeds were achieved. A dry cycle occurs when an engine is rotated on the starter motor without fuel or ignition, and is a normal check on initial installation. A wet cycle usually follows, the fuel being turned on but not the ignition; this serves the dual purpose of ensuring that the high pressure fuel cock operates correctly, and checks the engine and nacelle drainage, thus minimising the risk of fire.

A prolonged period of engine and aircraft system ground running followed, with particular attention being paid to the LP compressor drive shaft strain gauges. Since the engine had failed under the Vulcan test bed there had been several other failures, all equally catastrophic but fortunately confined to test beds. Despite a considerable research effort the cause of the shaft failure was not understood during this period.

The reheat system fitted to the Olympus 320 was a development of the innovative reheat unit first tested by the American Solar Company, and it proved extremely reliable. During the period of ground running at Boscombe Down, in over 1,200 attempts to select reheat, there was not one case of the reheat failing to light. We became used to the consistency of the reheat very quickly, so we were surprised when it sometimes failed to perform as advertised.

On initial selection of reheat only the pilot burner lit, the three spray rings being sequenced in by a distribution block as the throttle lever was advanced. To ensure that the fuel flow rates were consistent, valves were fitted in the distribution block so that each spray ring, or manifold, would be passing fuel at the correct rate and pressure before the next began to receive fuel.

On the day in question, the valve for the outer manifold failed to open during a slam acceleration to maximum reheat, and all the reheat fuel passed through the two inner manifolds. The fuel-air ratio was very high, and severe combustion instability occurred. To the surrounding engineers it sounded like a giant pneumatic drill.

The strain gauges on the LP drive shaft were constantly monitored by Test Measurement Department personnel during all ground runs in a nearby caravan because of the previously expressed doubts about the shaft integrity. Within a very short time Ray Gorrel of TMD reported that high stresses had been recorded, but in a torsional rather than diametral mode. The actual value of peak stress could not be accurately determined because the equipment was set for the latter mode. The recording gear was quickly reset, and the engine driver, Phil Pearce, advanced the throttle into reheat and the same hard 'pneumatic drill' sound occurred. The revised settings showed that torsional stresses of about 14 tons/sq.in. had been generated in the LP shaft by the reheat combustion instability.

It was thought at the time that the shaft had been permanently twisted, but careful measurements after the engine had been stripped failed to confirm that. The shaft was bent however, being .012 in. out of true at the worst point. Test bed running had shown prior to this that the shaft could be overloaded in torsion during reheat light ups, stresses of up to 4 tons/sq.in. being generated.

The overfuelling was temporarily prevented by fitting restrictors in the reheat fuel distribution block, but these had the additional effect of limiting the full clearance. A

MINISTRY OF AVIATION
AERONAUTICAL INSPECTION DIRECTORATE

To the Inspector-in-Charge, A.I.D.

at Bristol Evans,

APPLICATION FOR ENGINE RUN

In accordance with the requirements of Form 6/38, late Avmin Form 838, permission is requested for approved personnel to run

Engine No. 22218   Type Olympus
           22221   320.x

in Airframe No. X0219   Type TSR2

for the following purpose Engine Run, by B.S.E.

Date ....

Signed ....

For Messrs. BAC Weybridge

Approved ....
Inspector i/c, A.I.D.

Date 27. 9. 64

(1408) M724721 818 150 pds 12/52 TS&Co.Ltd. Gp.818   A.I.D. Form 28

*certified duplicate propellor carried out
1.A.W A.IS Concept '58*

R. Iredale

*Engines cleared for flight in accordance with:
F C Note 927 Issue 925
Amendment 15*

P.E.Brown

B.S.E.

This is a copy of the Form 1090, which was the application to the Aeronautical Inspection Directorate (AID, now known as the Aeronautical Quality Directorate, AQD), to clear the engines in the prototype TSR2 for its maiden flight. The author was in the rear seat for this run, and Phil Pearce, who signed for the engines on behalf of Bristol, was in the front.

[Rolls-Royce]

TSR2 takes-off from the main runway at RAF Boscombe Down on its maiden flight on 27 September 1964. The auxiliary intake doors were locked open for this flight, and the undercarriage was not retracted.

[*Rolls-Royce*]

MINISTRY OF AVIATION
AERONAUTICAL INSPECTION DIRECTORATE

To the Inspector-in-Charge, A.I.D.

at _Bristol Siddeley_

APPLICATION FOR ENGINE RUN

In accordance with the requirements of Form 6/38, late Avmin Form 838, permission is requested for approved personnel to run

Engine No. _22218_ / _22221_   Type _Olympus 320x_

in Airframe No. _XR219_   Type _TSR2_

for the following purpose _F-1090 —_ _Engine Run by B.S.E._

(Rep)

Date _[signature]_

Signed _J. A. Hammond_

For Messrs. _BAC Weybridge_

Approved _[signature]_ Inspector i/c, A.I.D.

Date _27. 9. 64_

(1405) M724721 818 150 pads 12/62 TSACo.Ltd. Gp.818   A.I.D. Form 28

certified duplicate propeller carried out

I.A.W A.I.S Curricula '58

[signature]

K. Iredale

Engines cleared for flight in accordance with

F C Note 927 in 925

Amendment 15

P. Pearce

_B S E_

This is a copy of the Form 1090, which was the application to the Aeronautical Inspection Directorate (AID, now known as the Aeronautical Quality Directorate, AQD), to clear the engines in the prototype TSR2 for its maiden flight. The author was in the rear seat for this run, and Phil Pearce, who signed for the engines on behalf of Bristol, was in the front.

[Rolls-Royce]

TSR2 takes-off from the main runway at RAF Boscombe Down on its maiden flight on 27 September 1964. The auxiliary intake doors were locked open for this flight, and the undercarriage was not retracted.

[*Rolls-Royce*]

92

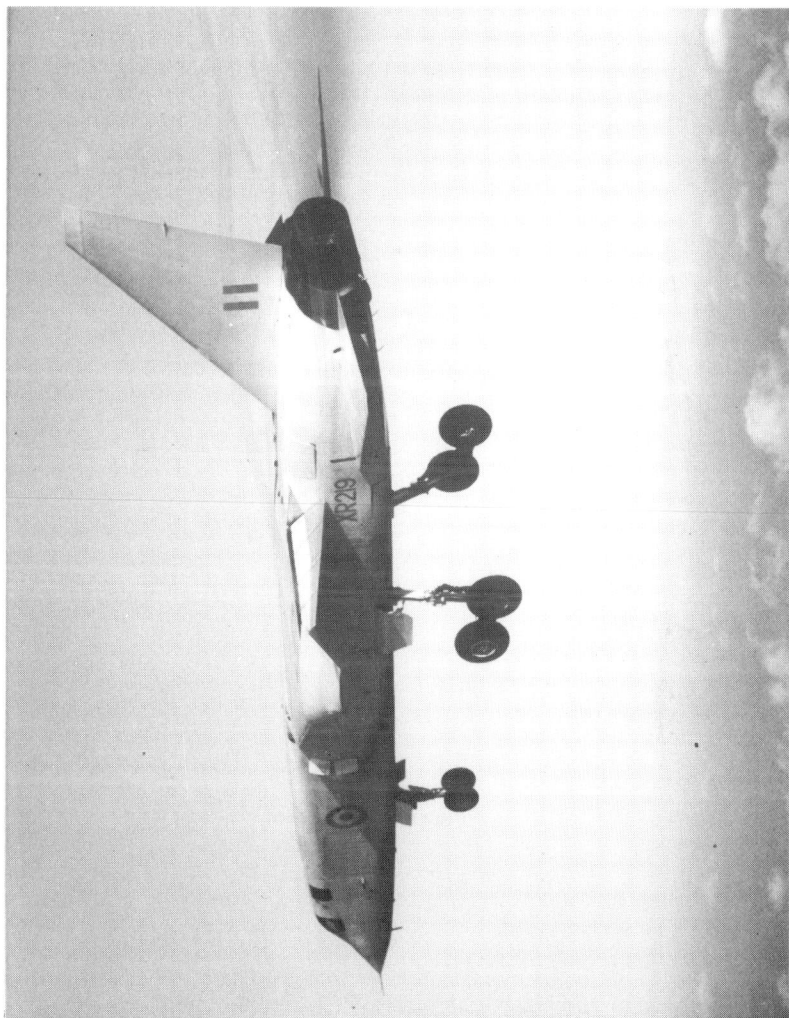

TSR2 on an early test flight, with the undercarriage down and the auxiliary intake doors locked open. The complex pattern of vortices from the drooped wing tips is worthy of note.
[*Rolls-Royce*]

93

design to introduce a flow proportioner system was under development, but had not flown before the project was cancelled. Subsequent reheat development showed that by reversing the reheat anvils and realigning the fuel manifolds, overfuelling could be accommodated without generating unacceptable shaft stresses.

During July 1964 320X number 2203 was carrying out a double 24 hour special category test on 103 bed at Patchway when the LP drive shaft failed, in the same manner as in the Vulcan incident, after some 50 hours running. The LP turbine disc was retained in the exhaust annulus, but the considerable damage resulted in the HP turbine disc being released. It circumnavigated the test bed several times, cutting through steel girders like a knife through butter. Such a failure in TSR2 would be catastrophic, possibly even allowing the crew insufficient time to escape, so it was decided to take the signals from the LP shaft strain gauges, amplify them and use the result to drive two red warning lights in the cockpit, one for each engine. Each light was set to illuminate if the shaft stress exceeded a certain value, which was set above the normal operating stress level.

One result of the continuing investigation into the shaft problem showed that the highest stresses occurred in the range 98 to 100% LP rpm. As a result the maximum permitted engine speed was reduced by 200 rpm for the first flight, and as a further precaution the engines were cleared for only one flight.

The technique of amplifying the signals from the strain gauges was fraught with problems. When signal levels were low, the system acted like a badly-tuned radio receiver and produced a lot of electrical 'noise'. There was a considerable risk that the noise could be amplified to trigger the warning in the absence of a genuine signal. When one considers that the illumination of the warning lights would be interpreted as saying that LP shaft failure was imminent, it can be seen that the implications of a false warning were more serious than usual.

One other, minor, problem dogged the engine runs. The main reheat fuel pump was a Dowty vapour core device. This had a centrifugal impeller that rotated at high speed. The fuel was introduced at the centre of the impeller, and because the pump ran dry when reheat was not in use, it was necessary to prime it before the reheat sequence could begin. This was achieved by running the pump on stall, or its maximum possible delivery pressure of about 2,000 lb/sq.in., until priming was complete. Under normal conditions the fuel pressure would drop to normal values as soon as the pump was primed, but occasionally the pump would stay on stall and consequently reheat fuel flows would be greater than expected. If both engines were selected to the same degree of reheat, and one pump stayed on stall, the resulting difference in fuel consumption would very quickly affect the trim of the aircraft. This intermittent problem stayed to the end of the project.

Engine running at Boscombe Down proceeded without a break for weekends or bank holidays. There was a tremendous urgency to get the aircraft flying, as we all knew the political climate was very uncertain. Consequently very large amounts of overtime were worked. This was particularly unfortunate for monthly staff, who at that time did not get paid for overtime. In the six months of the ground run phase, some individuals ran up over 600 hours, not making any allowance for premium time. Some engine runs were carried out at night. Reheat operation in the dark was a very spectacular event, as the flame was longer than the aircraft.

The account of the short flight test programme of TSR2 has been told by people better qualified than myself. This section will therefore confine itself to the engine behaviour in flight.

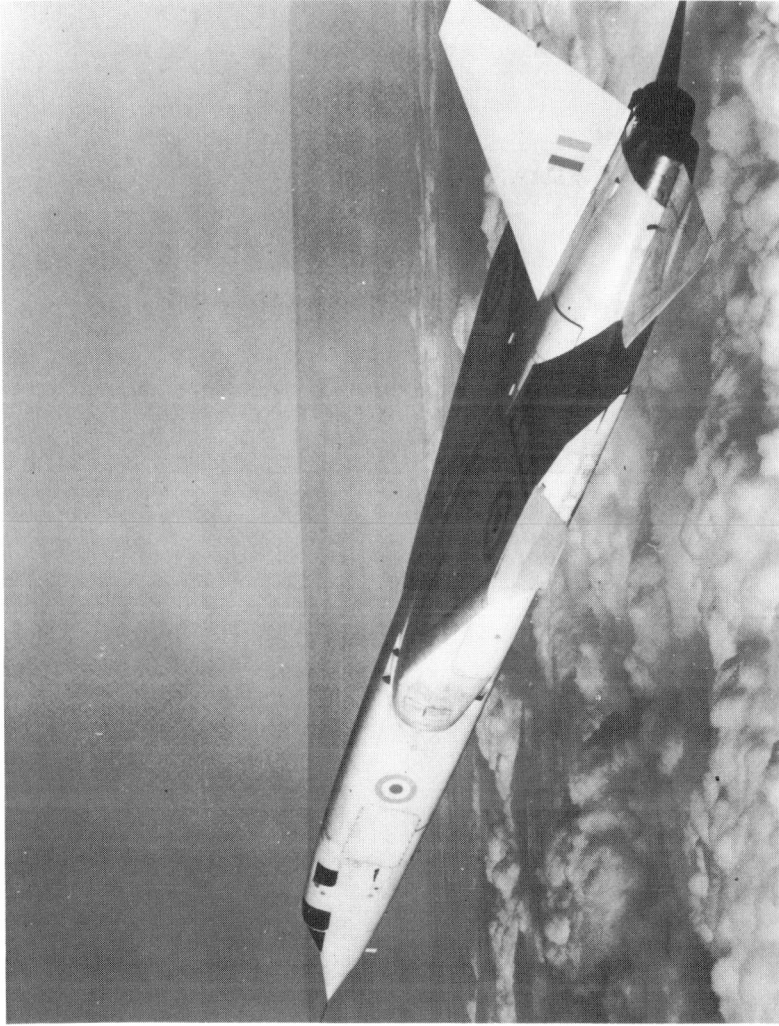

TSR2 pictured with undercarriage raised and the auxiliary intakes closed, which puts it on flight number ten at the earliest. The Bristol-manufactured rear fuselage fairing can be seen clearly.
[Rolls-Royce]

The first flight took place on 27 September 1964. The aircraft was captained by Wing Commander R P Beamont, DSO, OBE, DFC, with D J Bowen as navigator, no problems being experienced with the derated engines during the 14 minute flight. The engines had only been cleared for one flight, and it was not until 31 December that the second flight occurred with a replacement pair of engines.

On the second flight a severe vibration on the port engine resulted in an intolerable vibration being felt by Beamont whilst Bowen, sitting a few feet behind him, could feel nothing. A vibration analysis of the fuselage revealed that it possessed several antinodes, or points of maximum vibration, one of which coincided with the front cockpit. The vibration was later found to be caused by a defective pressurising spring within a low pressure fuel pump.

Flight 3 occurred on 2 January 1965, both the shaft over-stress warning lights illuminating when the aircraft was committed for take-off. Beamont correctly reasoned that the chance of both engines failing simultaneously was practically zero and continued with the take-off. He then flew a tight circuit and landed after a flight time of 8 minutes. There had been no high stresses in the shafts, the warnings had been triggered by random noise.

Initial attempts to raise the undercarriage in flight failed for a number of reasons, and the airspeed could not be increased much beyond 250 knots until the gear could be raised and lowered satisfactorily. After the third flight the port engine was changed, and the replacement did not produce any vibration. Flying proceeded in an attempt to cure the undercarriage problem, no further engine snags occurring until flight 8, when the port reheat pump stayed on stall following an inflight reheat selection. The same problem happened on the next flight during the reheat selection for take-off.

After flight 10 when the undercarriage was raised for the first time, the flight envelope rapidly expanded and by late February it was deemed adequate to allow the TSR2 to be transferred to Warton and on 22 February 1965 the ferry flight took place. Over the Irish Sea at 29,000 feet, 0.992 Indicated Mach Number was maintained with intermediate dry rating on both engines. The port engine was selected into reheat and the throttle slowly advanced to maximum. The aircraft was still accelerating and climbing when reheat was cancelled at 30,200 feet and 1.124 indicated Mach number. It was the first occasion when an Olympus went supersonic in level flight.

The reheat fuel pump remained on stall very occasionally during the next few flights, on one of which a maximum airspeed of 608 knots was attained. That corresponded to an intake ram pressure of 24.4 psi, probably the highest that an Olympus has ever experienced. The flight testing had concentrated on some aircraft flutter work and performance measurements at one of the guarantee points, 0.9 Mach Number at sea level. Very little dedicated engine testing was carried out.

The ultimate flight, number 24, was made on 31 March, bringing the total flight time to 13 hours 9 minutes. 23 flights had been achieved in 12 weeks, a high rate of flying for a first prototype at the very start of its programme. Very little in the way of snags had delayed the testing at Warton, a level of serviceability that was quite outstanding.

Before XR219 was transferred to Warton, XR220, the second prototype arrived at Boscombe Down on the back of an articulated lorry. Whilst manoeuvring the vehicle into the hangar, the driver somehow managed to get the tractor at right angles to the trailer. The whole thing tipped over on to its side, and the fuselage of XR220 partially slid off the lorry, coming to rest with most of its weight taken on one of the taileron pintles. It was repaired, although the fuselage had to be rejigged and checked for trueness. By the time the project was cancelled, it had completed all the necessary ground run checks, and was very close to obtaining flight clearance.

TSR2 being towed out for a ground run, probably at British Aircraft Corporation's (now British Aerospace) airfield at Warton, near Blackpool. Compare the size of these nozzles with those for the Olympus 101 shown in Chapter Two.

[*Rolls-Royce*]

BAC very quickly produced a proposal to use the prototype for a limited research programme to evaluate the design criteria of the aircraft, at a cost of some two million pounds. The tests would have explored the planned flight envelope, and would have provided BAC and BSEL with a significant amount of data on supersonic flight, much of which could have been read across to the proposed supersonic transport. The Government was only prepared to consider the plan if BAC were prepared to allow the costs to be debitted to the cancellation dues, and this they were in no position to do.

The mechanism of the vibration problem in the LP compressor drive shaft was understood before the cancellation. The major source of excitation was traced to an air leak through the rear location of the HP compressor rotor air transfer tube caused by differential growth and slight collapse of the tube. This caused an air pressure oscillation in the inter-shaft cavity which was in resonance with the shaft itself. An initial cure consisted of shrinking two rings on to the centre section of the shaft. These did not prevent the resonance but restricted the resulting vibration. Shafts to this standard appeared too late to be used in the aircraft. The HP air tube was also redesigned with a conical extension, and this was shown to produce no significant vibration.

Whilst the TSR2 was still extant Lionel Haworth, the Chief Designer, had been so worried about the LP shaft situation that he designed a two-piece bolted shaft incorporating 'pennies' in the centre section, the pennies and the bolted flange providing a measure of inbuilt damping that was absent in the original design. Cancellation prevented the redesign from being tested in a 320.

The Bristol contribution to TSR2 extended literally beyond its engines, as BSEL also manufactured the fuselage rear fairing. This was fabricated out of Waspalloy, a very intractable material in which to work. The fairing can clearly be seen in photographs as the section in natural metal finish at the rear of the fuselage.

It may seem, on reading this chapter, that undue space has been devoted to the mechanical problems that beset the engine. From an engineering point of view, it is the failures that provide the interest, that fill in the points on the learning curve, so to speak. From the beginning the engine showed enormous potential, a fact that was recognised by four other firms who also produced responses to OR339. Avro, de Havilland, Bristol and Hawker all had proposals specifying the B.01 22R or a close derivative. The promise of the 22R was ultimately realised in the Olympus 593 series of engines, the story of which is recounted in Chapter 5.

There was to be no dignity for the airframes. XR219, the only one to fly, was transported to Proof and Experimental Establishment Foulness Island along with XR221, which was 90% complete, the purpose being to ascertain the effect of shell and rocket impact upon milled aircraft structures. XR220 initially went to RAF Henlow, being allocated the instructional serial 7933M. A belated realisation that TSR2 represented a significant milestone in aviation progress in this country resulted in XR220 being presented to the Cosford Air and Space Museum. XR222, another virtually complete machine, was put on display at the Imperial War Museum, Duxford, and has since been restored to pristine condition.

The cancellation of TSR2 did not mark the end of work on the Olympus 320. Three engines continued running for many years at NGTE Pyestock, engaged in a programme to develop a digital engine control system which was jointly controlled by Bristol, NGTE and Elliott Flight Automation. One of the engines used, which had originally flown in the starboard nacelle of XR219, tolerated over 400 surges in the course of 200

An Olympus Mark 320 in Number 2 shop. This mark of engine was rated at 30,610 pounds thrust at take-off, including reheat.
[Rolls-Royce]

hours testing during the programme without displaying any damage or failure whatsoever. A further NGTE study into the mechanism of engine surge also used a 320, chosen mainly because of its ability to tolerate many surges without damage, a characteristic of all the members of the Olympus family.

The design of the Olympus 320, and its subsequent, at times difficult, development made significant advances in the understanding of many aspects of gas turbine technology. It is therefore fitting that an example has been preserved in the Science Museum in London.

4. Industrial and Marine

All at Sea

When the gas turbine first became available for aircraft, it rapidly supplanted the piston engine, mainly because it enabled the designers to get rid of propeller drag and it consequently opened up a range of airspeeds that was out of reach of propeller driven aircraft. At first the gas turbine was seen to provide similar advantages for light, fast Naval patrol craft and as a result the first all-gas-turbine boat in the Royal Navy, and the world, was HMS *Grey Goose*. Powered by two purpose-built Rolls-Royce RM60s, she went to sea in 1953, following on from other experimental craft.

The light weight of the gas turbine provided another convincing argument for their use in light craft. It was thought, however, that in the larger ocean-going warships where machinery weight was not a major problem, reductions in the weight of the engine could introduce problems of stability, as weight would be reduced low down in the hull. At a time when ships were proliferating bigger and heavier radar aerials, this was considered a positive disadvantage.

The overriding reason for the initial use of gas turbines in ships was the rapidity that maximum power could be achieved from cold. There was no need for a ship to keep steam at short notice. Later it became apparent that there was another, equally valid, argument in favour of the gas turbine and that was the almost complete lack of maintenance. There was a dramatic reduction in onboard maintenance work, and the manning and training requirement consequently diminished, along with a vastly increased reliability. It has been calculated that the gas turbine requires only one quarter of the man hours needed for maintenance of steam or diesel machinery of equivalent power output.

Two other early criticisms have turned into major selling points. The high-profile use of gas turbines is in aviation, and in that field they are noticeably noisy, despite recent improvements. In the 1950s they were exceptionally noisy, produced vast amounts of dirty, smelly exhaust fumes, and were considered too fragile for Naval use, because it was known that one small bird could wreck an aero engine. The main source of noise from the airborne gas turbine is of course from the high velocity exhaust gas, whereas the maritime gas turbine has most of the energy of the jet removed by the power turbine. As a further plus, there were virtually no machinery noises from the gas turbine. As a consequence the sound of the jet is lost in the normal shipboard noises of wind and water, and the gas turbine offers a significant reduction in underwater noise generation, making ships more difficult to detect by sonar.

The supposed fragility of the aero gas turbine was quite another matter. A ship crashing through heavy seas can generate shock loads of 30g or more, and it was not thought that a light weight power plant could possibly have the ruggedness required of a marine engine. However, aero engines are designed to cope with high stress loads and the thermal shocks generated in going from idle to full power in a matter of seconds. With the appropriate strengthening of casings and mounting structure, the gas turbine has shown itself more than capable of withstanding shock loadings in excess of 30g. Naval trials have in fact shown that exceptionally brief accelerations as high as 300g can be tolerated.

The Olympus was the second Bristol engine to be 'marinised' for ship propulsion, the first being the Proteus. Many vital lessons were learned on the Proteus installations, which were used in a range of fast patrol craft, hovercraft and hydrofoils, and are still in use on the 'Mountbatten' class of cross-channel hovercraft and many patrol boats.

The first marine Olympus was built for the German Navy. Bristol had already made studies of an installation with an initial rating of 22,000 shp, but did not wish to commit design effort for what might prove to be a one-off. Brown Boveri were brought in as partners, and after two years of preliminary design, in May 1962, the German Ministry of Defence awarded a contract to Bristol Siddeley for the marinised gas generator and to Brown Boveri for a new design of two-stage long-life marine power turbine, complete with engine mounting arrangements.

In 1965 the engine passed its acceptance tests at Mannheim and it was delivered to the Navy's technical establishment at Kiel, where a new test bed had been built for extended shore trials. In the meantime, work was proceeding on the design of a new class of gas turbine frigate. In the event the Ministry abandoned the construction of the new ship, ordering American- built Charles F Adams class destroyers instead.

In 1968 the Finnish Navy commissioned two 700 ton corvettes which were to be named *Turunmaa* and *Karjalla*. The *Turunmaa* was the first ship to operate an Olympus at sea, beginning its trials early in 1968, six months before HMS *Exmouth*, the first British ship. The Finnish ships were powered by a single Olympus of 22,000 shp on the centre shaft, supplemented by a diesel and with a 1200 hp Mercedes Benz diesel on each wing shaft in a CODAG arrangement. The diesels were capable of independent operation.

Experience gained in industrial applications such as Hams Hall power station and elsewhere, and marine operations with Proteus and the solitary Olympus in the German Navy's test stand, clearly identified the changes that had to be made. Changes in the materials used were straightforward in the compressor section, where magnesium casings were changed to aluminium because it was known that magnesium reacts with sea water, and aluminium compressor blading was changed to stainless steel and then to titanium. Other modifications were in the combustion chambers where units were to run on diesel fuel in an attempt to reduce the smoke emission. This effort was ultimately successful, although it took several years.

The power turbine was considerably revised from the earlier Brown Boveri two-stage version. The Royal Navy choice consisted of a single stage operating at 5,660 rpm utilising wide chord blades and overhung from a rear-facing shaft so that the plain bearings were out of the hot gas stream and available for inspection.

In 1966 Rolls-Royce acquired BSEL, so perhaps from this point on it would be proper to use the current designation. The first Rolls-Royce marine Olympus started running on the test bed in August 1966 and continued for the next two years, when the first seagoing unit went into service. When the initial decision to adopt the Olympus

The Finnish Navy corvette *Turunmaa*, which was the first Olympus-powered warship to enter service with any navy. Recently refurbished, she and her sister-ship *Karjalla* are expected to remain in service until the year 2005. [*Rolls-Royce*]

had been taken by the Ministry of Defence in 1964, the intention had been to use a pair of Olympus TM1As rated at 22,300 shp as boost engines in a COSAG arrangement for the new Type 82 Destroyers, the sole example of which, HMS *Bristol*, was ordered in 1966. In order to get early sea experience of the new engine, it was decided to convert an existing steam powered Blackwood class frigate, HMS *Exmouth*, and it was in this ship that sea trials started in 1968.

In 1967 the Ministry of Defence had finally decided to use gas turbine propulsion for a range of new frigates and destroyers and in 1968 the Ministry awarded a design contract for a frigate to Vosper Thorneycroft and Yarrow. Vosper had secured a contract in 1966 for four small destroyers for the Iranian Navy, which were to be powered by Olympus CODOG machinery, while Yarrow had a contract six months earlier for a Malaysian Navy frigate, also with Olympus CODOG machinery. The *Saam* class frigates built for the Iranian Navy displaced about 1200 tons compared with the 1800 tons of the Yarrow frigates, but they were equipped with two Olympus' and Paxman diesels. They cruised at 18 knots and were capable of 39 knots in the half fuel condition. In the Yarrow design the machinery consisted of a single Olympus giving a speed of 27 knots and a Crossley Pielstock diesel giving a speed of 16 knots. Instead of mounting both engines on the centre line feeding on to a single shaft, Yarrow produced a twin-screw arrangement, with the gas turbine and diesel feeding through clutches into a common gearbox with a split output. *Exmouth*, in contrast, had the conventional single shaft layout.

The *Exmouth* conversion utilised two Proteus units rated at 3,600 shp each, both being mounted on the after side of the main gearbox, and a marine Olympus TM1 downrated to 15,000 shp in a COGOG arrangement. On 5 July 1968, *Exmouth* started sea trials as the worlds first major warship to have all gas turbine power. Just nine days later after 64 hours running the Olympus engine suffered the complete failure of the first row of LP compressor blades, and the trial was abruptly halted.

This failure was not easy to understand, as by 1968 some 27,000 hours had been logged by the considerable number of industrial engines in service. Some industrial Olympus engines had exceeded 1,000 hours, and all used the same stainless steel compressor blades. Careful analysis showed that the blades had not failed as a result of foreign object damage, but had failed in fatigue caused by excessive blade vibration. That implied that an installation effect lay at the cause of the failure. A likely area for investigation was the air inlet trunking, so a series of exact scale models, based upon actual measurements taken from the *Exmouth* installation, was made. These ranged from a one-fifth scale model used for water analogue tests to a full-sized replica for use as an engine test bed, the latter being equipped with instrumentation rakes to measure air pressure and temperature at various stations in the inlet.

The cause of the failure soon became clear. The air inlet trunking had to be built into an existing ship, and in the process had acquired an asymmetric shape. This had caused a flow break away at the bottom of the vertical section on one side only, producing a stagnant zone at about four o'clock on the compressor face. The first-stage compressor blades thus suffered a complete load reversal once every revolution.

Within the confines of a ship's hull it is never possible to guarantee the design of the air inlet ducting such that perfectly smooth, laminar flow air can be supplied at the engine face. The possibility of damage due to enemy action further renders this ideal unobtainable. The alternative was to smooth the air at the engine face, after it had passed through the various sections of intake trunking imposed by the hull design.

HMS *Exmouth* was the first Royal Navy ship to use a marine-Olympus, installed in conjunction with a marine-Proteus in a COGOG arrangement. Exmouth did valuable work as an FTB - floating test bed - in proving the concept of the gas turbine as a sea-going powerplant.

[*Rolls-Royce*]

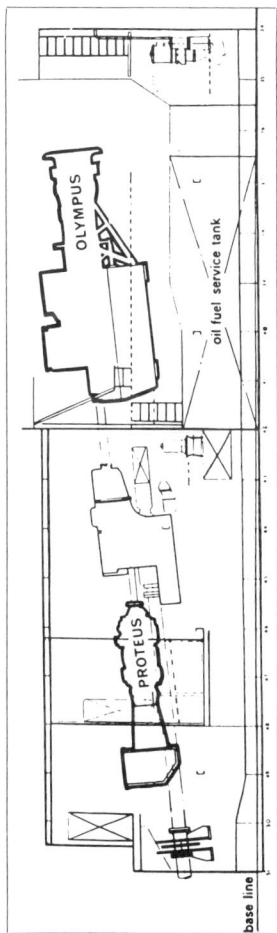

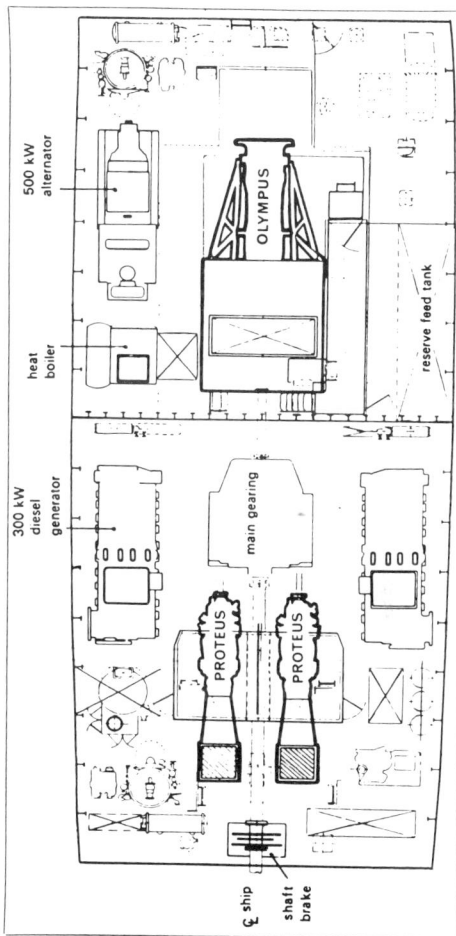

The arrangement of the all-gas-turbine machinery which was installed in HMS *Exmouth*. It brought the advantage of a compact installation and permitted automation to be effectively introduced.

[*Rolls-Royce*]

Labels in diagram: OLYMPUS, PROTEUS, oil fuel service tank, base line, 500 kW alternator, 300 kW diesel generator, heat boiler, reserve feed tank, main gearing, ℄ ship, shaft brake

The Vosper Mark 7 frigate, *Dat Assawari*, was ordered by the Libyan Navy in 1968. She is powered by two Olympus' and two Paxman diesels in a CODOG arrangement. She is capable of 39 knots under Olympus power, and has a cruising speed of 18 knots.

[*Rolls-Royce*]

With flow straighteners in the form of a cascaded duct installed, and the engine rebuilt, trials resumed on 15 October. The subsequent tests proceeded smoothly, and the flow straighteners subsequently became a standard feature of all later engine installations.

The initial marine Olympus in its TM1A form produced 22,300 shp, but naval architects could already envisage requirements of 28,000 shp. This would have involved turbine entry temperatures well above the level at which uncooled blades could be used; the TM1A when operated at 24,000 shp had a TET of 1155°K, whereas 28,000 shp would involve temperatures around 1220°K. To achieve this power output a relatively simple degree of blade cooling—on the first row of stators only—was introduced.

Along with these improvements the overall power requirements of the future fleet were examined. It was found possible to produce an almost standard Main Propulsion Machinery Package, using Olympus and Tyne engines in a COGOG arrangement. In this form it was used for the first time in the Type 21 Frigate, of which HMS *Amazon* was the class leader, and which proved extremely popular with their crews.

The output speeds of the two engines were quite different. The Olympus, generating 28,000 shp had its power turbine turning at 5,660 rpm while the smaller Tyne generated 4,250 shp at 12,750 rpm. In order to match these speeds more closely, the Tyne was geared down through a small primary gearbox, built as part of the Tyne module.

The problem of providing astern power had been evident from the first sea going trials of the gas turbine. Reversing gearboxes had been used, but the techniques were very different in view of the high transmitted loads, and similarly controllable pitch propellers were initially looked upon with disfavour, although they later became standard. So, in 1967 Rolls-Royce produced a highly ingenious proposal for a reversing Olympus.

This consisted of a standard gas generator coupled to a centripetal, or inward flow, turbine. This was fitted with swivelling nozzles which could be rotated to give ahead or astern power to the impeller. A third-scale model was built and operated as a cold flow rig, but overall complications of size, weight and efficiency could not easily be overcome, and the idea was shelved.

In 1972, a year after a formal agreement was signed between Rolls-Royce and Kawasaki Heavy Industries of Japan, a complete Olympus module was shipped to Kawasaki's Kobe factory. It was supplied for demonstration use, and was followed by the first orders for ship sets in 1977. The *Hatsuyuki* class destroyer was powered by the twin Olympus/Tyne configuration, and the *Ishikari* class, the first new Japanese frigate design since the mid-1960s, employed a single Olympus in conjunction with a diesel engine for cruising. Progressively more engine manufacture was undertaken in Japan until the Japanese content was roughly 75%, with the remainder supplied in kit form from the UK.

The 100th marine Olympus was produced at Ansty in August 1978, and was installed in HMS *Nottingham*, a Type 42 frigate.

As more seagoing experience was gained with the marine gas turbine, the size of vessel that it was applied to grew. In May 1977 HMS *Invincible* became the biggest ship in the world to have all gas turbine propulsion. She was the first of a new class of mini-carrier, although she was at first described as a through-deck cruiser, and at a displacement of 19,500 tons was less than half the displacement of the Navy's previous big (fleet) carrier, Ark Royal.

The propulsion machinery for *Invincible* consists of four Olympus TM3B modules mounted in a COGAG arrangement, giving a total power output in excess of 100,000

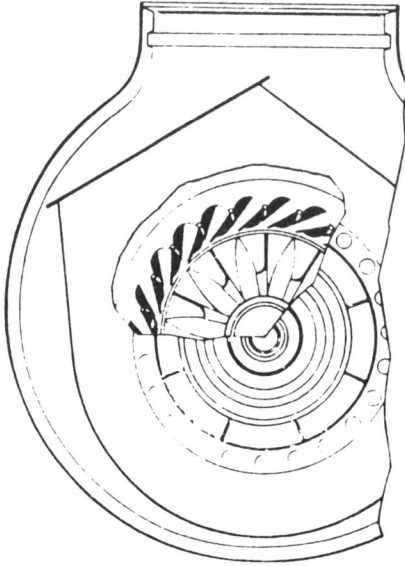

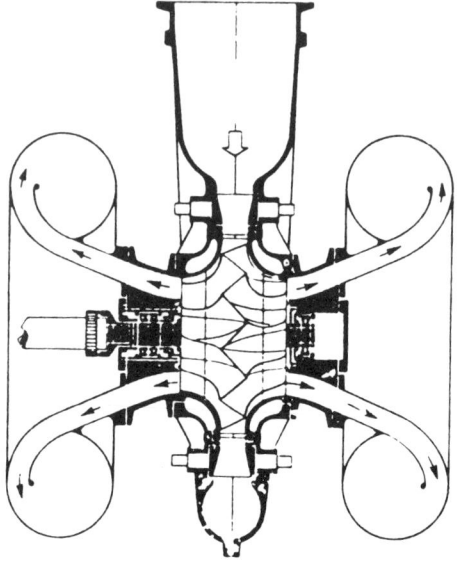

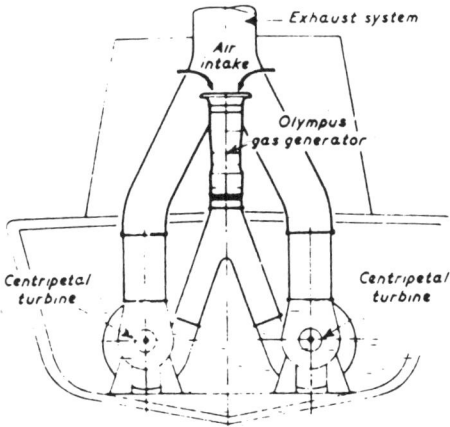

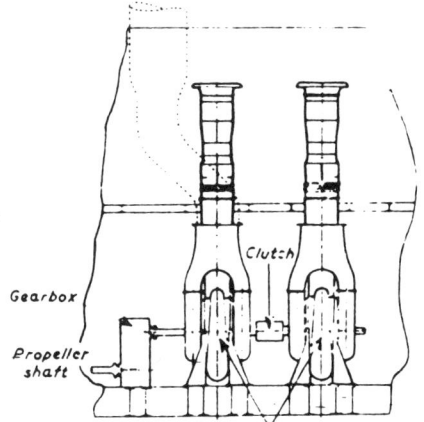

The centripetal, or inward flow, turbine, which was a laudable but still-born attempt to produce a reversing Olympus. Reversing gears or controllable-pitch propellers still provide the best solution to the problem of manoeuvring.   [*Rolls-Royce*]

shp. Each complete TM3B module consists of the air intake, gas generator and power turbine. One engine in each pair is fed by air from intakes on the port side and the other receives its air from starboard intakes. Before entering the engine the air is passed through a filtration and spray separation system. Engine pairs drive through a David Brown triple reduction and reversing gearbox. The drive can be reversed without stopping the engines, as a combination of fluid couplings and a self-shifting clutch is employed.

Rolls-Royce built a close replica of a twin-Olympus installation at Ansty to test the intakes and uptake trunking and gearboxes, and utilised a Froude dynamometer to apply typical loadings. The facility began operating in 1973, and a large amount of engine running had been achieved by the time Invincible was launched.

When she joined the Navy, in early 1980, she was accepted by Captain Michael Livesy, who signed for the ship on behalf of the Admiralty. Her Chief Engineer, Lieutenant-Commander Peter Clarke, said of the Olympus engines, "They are magnificent. You just select a button and there's all that power—instantly." Lt-Cdr Clarke had previously spent four years with steam turbines in Ark Royal. "Here there's no need for anything to get dirty—and no one to make it so.", he said. "Ark Royal's watch below consisted of 88 men. We have 11."

The almost exclusively Rolls-Royce-powered Invincible, taking into account its complement of Sea Harriers as well as its helicopters, Sea Dart missiles and its main propulsion equipment, soon acquired the soubriquet of 'HMS *Rolls-Royce.*'

In 1982 Argentine troops occupied the Falkland Islands and South Georgia, precipitating the largest combined operation by British forces since the end of the Second World War. Operation Corporate, the action to retake the Islands, was the first conflict involving large numbers of warships powered by gas turbines. Nineteen of the Royal Navy's major units were propelled by Rolls-Royce marine gas turbines. Throughout the campaign, no engine had to be changed during the period of hostilities as a result of mechanical failure, and no ship was withdrawn because of a defective main propulsion system.

At the beginning of Corporate, most of the naval ships that were to become involved were in home ports. Unfortunately, the Olympus modules in *Invincible* were approaching the end of their planned overhaul life. Rolls-Royce immediately increased the on-condition life of its gas turbines by 500 hours and instituted a policy of partial maintenance so that any engine could be restored to a 2,000 hour life within 35 days.

Before Operation Corporate the intention had been for engine changes to be carried out in harbour with full dockyard facilities readily available. When a long campaign stretching through the Antarctic winter was seen as likely, it was recognised that it might become necessary to replace engines whilst on station. In COGOG ships the Olympus and Tyne gas generators are inserted and removed via their intakes. Clearances are tight and land-based assistance had been thought to be necessary. However the operational situation soon brought about a change of these opinions, and routines were devised for engine changes at sea.

The plans for the frigates were never to be tested in practice during the war. It was left to HMS *Invincible* after five months continuously on station to carry out the first engine change at sea. Unlike the smaller ships, *Invincible* carries two spare gas generators permanently on board, slung in the engine room in pods. The exit route for the unit is not via its intake, but across the engine room on a trolley and up to the hangar deck on one of the lifts. The critical period occurs when the engine is being transferred to its trolley, when it is suspended from a crane and must be restrained to cushion ship

HMS *Bristol* is powered by steam turbines, with two Olympus TM1As for high-speed dash, in a COSAG arrangement. She represents an interim design between the steam-turbine and the all-gas-turbine powered vessels. She is the first, and only, Type 82 destroyer and was originally tasked with the duties of carrier escort. What a pity HMS *Olympus* was a diesel-electric submarine, and not a ship like this. [Rolls-Royce]

The Royal Hellenic Navy frigate HS *Limnos* is powered by a standard Royal Navy machinery package of two Olympus' and two Tynes in a COGOG arrangement.

[*Rolls-Royce*]

HMS *Amazon*, the first ship in her class, at speed. Amazon, a Type 21 frigate, is powered by Olympus TM1 and Tyne gas turbines in a COGOG arrangement.

[*Crown Copyright*]

The Royal Thailand Navy ship *Makut Rajakumarn* is a Yarrow-built Y-type frigate powered by a single Olympus, giving a speed of 27 knots, and a Crossley-Pielstick diesel which gives a cruising speed of 16 knots, in a CODOG arrangement. [*Rolls-Royce.*]

HMS *Cardiff*, a *Sheffield*-class Type 42 destroyer, is powered by a twin Olympus/Twin Tyne machinery set in a COGOG arrangement. The lead ship of the class, HMS *Sheffield*, sank as a result of damage caused by an Argentinian Exocet missile on 4 May 1982. Her Olympus engines thus became the first to be lost due to enemy action.

[Crown Copyright]

movement. Machinery and personnel are particularly vulnerable during this phase. Undaunted by the difficulties, in the month following the end of hositilities the engineering staff of HMS *Invincible* changed two time-expired Olympus engines at sea with complete success. HMS *Invincible* was at sea, fully operational, for a total of 166 days, a phenomenal achievement that says a great deal for the reliability of the Olympus and the viability of the four-engined COGAG installation.

When the gas turbine was first considered for maritime use, concern was expressed about the apparent fragility of the device. Action damage sustained during air attack showed that the gas turbine was well able to withstand shock damage. HMS *Glasgow*, a Type 42 frigate powered by two Olympus and two Tyne engines was hit by a bomb which passed through the after engine-room, partially flooding it. Both Tynes were put out of action because of severe damage to their intake transition pieces, although they could have been operated in an emergency by taking suction from the machinery space and accepting the risk of foreign object damage to their compressors from the shattered trunking. This was not necessary however, as both Olympus engines in the forward engine room remained fully available, enabling the ship to manoeuvre as normal. Once the fires had been extinguished, the intakes of both Tynes were repaired locally, one with wood and the other by welding. HMS *Glasgow* remained available for action at all times. In contrast, a steam-powered vessel, HMS *Argonaut*, was out of action for over four hours after a similar bomb hit, because of shock loading of the steam turbines.

Fleet-wide use of the Olympus used in the boost role for high speed dash in the Type 21, 22 and 42 vessels increased by a factor of four during the Falklands Conflict when compared with the same period in 1981, indicating the value of the rapid response of a gas turbine in getting a ship out of danger or in pressing home an attack.

In 1985 the Finnish patrol vessel *Turunmaa* was refurbished and recommissioned, with the expectation of a further fifteen years of service. The *Turunmaa* originally entered service in 1967, becoming the first Olympus-powered warship to do so. She was followed by a sister-ship, the *Karjalla*, which was also refurbished and returned to service in 1986. The upgrading included fitting the latest standard of fuel system and an up-to-date digital control system. Both vessels returned to service in the Baltic, where they had spent all their previous sea time.

The last two Olympus engines to enter service with the Royal Navy did so in the Type 22 destroyer HMS *Coventry*, named after the Type 42 frigate of the same name that was lost during the bitter air-sea battles of 1982. Subsequent ships will be fitted with a Tyne/Spey configuration. The new HMS *Coventry* is the sixth ship in the Royal Navy to carry the name.

In 1988 a pair of Olympus Mark 2017 engines were removed from the Royal Netherlands Navy ships *Tromp* and *De Ruyter* after more than a decade of use. Both engines had achieved more than 100,000 miles 'on the clock' at the time of removal. The engine from *Tromp* had been installed for 12 years and had completed over 4,000 hours operation, whilst that from *De Ruyter* had completed 3,800 hours in 11 years. Neither gas generator showed much wear.

Today the Olympus is perhaps the most widely used of the marine gas turbines, being installed in eighteen different classes of vessel ranging from the 700-ton *Turunmaa* of the Finnish Navy to the pride and joy of the Royal Navy, the 19,500-ton aircraft carrier, HMS *Invincible*. In total, about 250 marine Olympus engines have been sold to 16 navies to be installed in over 100 ships.

HMS *Invincible*, otherwise known as 'HMS *Rolls-Royce*'. The four rectangular openings visible in the side of the hull, two ahead and two behind the lifeboat compartment, are air intakes for the Olympus engines. There are identical openings on the starboard side.

[*Crown Copyright*]

Two Type 21 frigates In the foreground is HMS *Antelope*, which was sunk in San Carlos Water during the landings on the Falkland Islands. [*Rolls-Royce*]

H.M.S. ARK ROYAL

HMS *Ark Royal*, an Invincible-class aircraft carrier, is powered by four Olympus gas turbines in a COGAG arrangement Sea Harriers (Rolls-Royce Pegasus engines) can be seen ranged on the flight-deck, and the ski-jump is much in evidence.

[*Rolls-Royce*]

Power for the People

The Olympus first went into service as an industrial power generator in late 1962, when the Central Electricity Generating Board (CEGB) commissioned a single prototype engine at their Hams Hall power station near Birmingham. Proteus-powered generating sets with an ouput of 2.7 Megawatts (MW) had been in use since 1959, but their use was confined to the more remote 'end of the line' part of the system, and to some overseas plant.

An Olympus 15 megawatt installation, similar to the Hams Hall power station generating set. The large ducting seen at the rear of the engine removed the power turbine exhaust.   [*Rolls-Royce*]

The CEGB's first essay with the Olympus was a tentative effort, made rather because the gas turbine looked attractive economically as a peak load machine than in response to any real need. Indeed, an earlier survey carried out by a market research organisation demonstrated pretty conclusively that there was no market at all for such a device. Fortunately, before this depressing prediction had any practical effect, both Bristol Siddeley and the electrical companies English Electric and AEI, were deluged with orders from the CEGB to the tune of 1464 MW in 1962/3 alone.

To be fair to the market researchers, few people had foreseen either the extent to which gas turbine plant would be used to fill the gaps at short notice in an expanding electrical supply system, or the stimulus they would receive from the major power failure in Britain in 1964, and the more serious East Coast blackout in the USA the following year.

The Hams Hall installation used an Olympus 201 gas generator, exhausting through a two-stage turbine. Power was transmitted from the free power turbine to a Brush alternator through a gear type coupling shaft. Provision was also made for a clutch to be fitted if the alternator was to be used as a synchronous condenser. The engine was adapted to run on a wide range of fuels, initially kerosine, diesel and later natural gas when it became available. After passing through the turbine the exhaust gases were further diffused to a low velocity by flowing through an exhaust volute before being discharged to atmosphere.

The Brush synchronous alternator had an output of 20 MW at 3000 rpm. It was 23 feet 6 inches long and 16 feet 8 inches wide and weighed 70 tons. It was directly air cooled, and one interesting aspect of the installation was that special foundations were required for the alternator but not for the Olympus. The installation was capable of a very quick run up and could be on full load within 2 to 3 minutes of starting up. Prior to the installation at Hams Hall, a series of tests were completed at Ansty at loads of up to a quarter of full power. That was sufficient for load rejection overspeed tests to be made, and to assess the power turbine operation. In addition, strain gauge measurements were made on blades and discs.

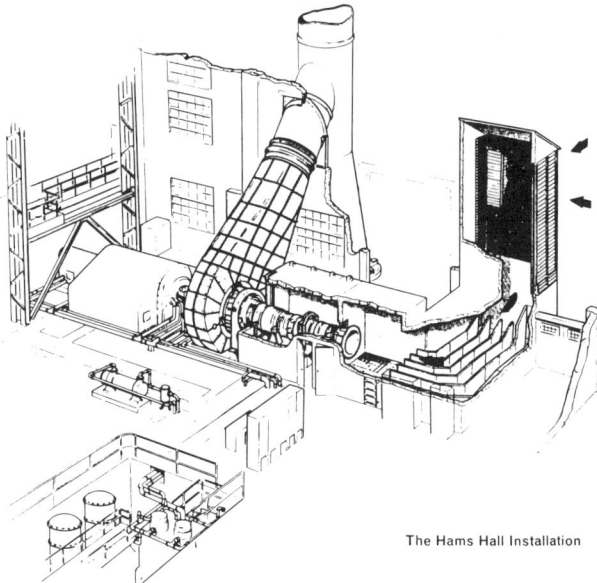

The Hams Hall Installation

A cutaway view of the Olympus installation in the Hams Hall power station.   [*Rolls-Royce*]

It is one of the characteristics of a gas generator that it produces more power as the air inlet temperature falls. This feature is ideal for peak lopping as power demand naturally increases with a drop in temperature, so the highest power output is available when the requirement is greatest.

Early checks were minimal on the installed unit. Engine oil and fuel filters were examined every month or 100 hours running, and automatic compressor washes were carried out to maintain efficiency.

The set was readily adaptable to remote control, and once initiated the battery driven starter turned the engine and began an automatic starting sequence. After 25 seconds the engine lit, became self-sustaining and ran up to idling speed.

When idle was reached the automatic sequence continued to open the throttle until the power turbine speed approached that needed for synchronising the alternator output with the mains supply, at 50 Hz. The governor was adjusted until the alternator attained 51 Hz. It was then reduced and the precise speed at which it was synchronised with the mains frequency determined by a synchronising unit. The governor datum was then opened to 100% and the throttle opened to give maximum power.

When the extra generation capacity was no longer required, the run-down was similarly automatic. After five minutes at idle the engine was stopped.

Low operational noise was maintained by careful design of the inlet and exhaust ducting. Air was drawn into the gas generator through a duct of approximately 85 square feet area housing sound absorbent splitters. Air discharged from the power turbine was ducted from the exhaust volute to a vertical silencer. As a result the level of noise audible outside the plant was considered acceptable for use in residential areas.

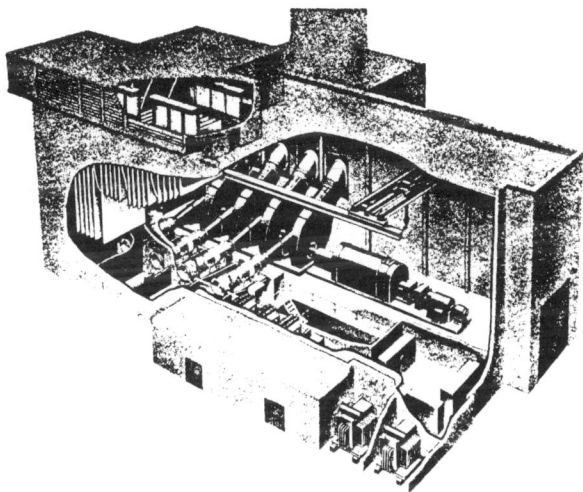

A cutaway view of a typical quadruple-Olympus installation, which under the right conditions could produce 80 megawatts of electricity.
[*Rolls-Royce*]

The basic set consisted of a single Olympus plus alternator, but also on offer were twin units of double the output, and quadruple units that offered 70/80 MW.

Orders continued to flow in. In the spring of 1964, for example, the CEGB ordered six basic Olympus generating sets. Four of these went into Ratcliffe Hall power station in Nottinghamshire and two went into the Ironbridge power station in Shropshire. The order was worth two million pounds at the time and raised the total number of Olympus sets ordered and commissioned to 32.

The first overseas site for the Olympus-powered generating set was on Jersey. The 17.5/20 megawatt set was ordered by the General Electric Company for the Jersey Electrical Company, and was installed at the Queens Road Power Station, St Helier, which has the distinction of being the largest diesel generating station in Europe, with a capacity of 50 megawatts. The Olympus set, which was commissioned in 1963, can be started either manually or automatically, and can be synchronised within two minutes of the commencement of the starting sequence. It was installed mainly to provide extra generating capacity for the summer months, when the influx of visitors greatly increases the demand for power.

The site manager at Jersey, Allan Deakin, had an interesting experience one day while waiting at the docks for some urgently needed parts. His vigil was interrupted by a Royal Navy officer who asked him if he would mind having a look at his ship, which turned out to be one of the then new marine-Proteus powered fast patrol boats. One of the engines had developed a fault which Deakin, with his engineering background, was able to identify and put right. It was some time before the Navy discovered how the Company had managed to react so quickly to their request for help.

Almost a quarter of a century later, in 1986, a second Olympus SK30 set was commissioned in the Queens Road Power Station, taking its place alongside the first which is still in use.

In the spring of 1966, further orders were received for the basic Olympus set, one being required for installation in the Canary Islands to supplement the three Proteus generating sets there. During the twelve months that were required to complete the installation, two further 2.7 MW sets were leased to the authorities. Since then the Olympus has been progressively uprated.

The Cowes, Isle of Wight, power station. It can generate a total of 140 megawatts from eight Olympus sets, and is used for peak lopping in the summer, when the influx of holidaymakers doubles the indigenous population.   [Rolls-Royce]

122

The operation of a modern gas turbine power station is exemplified by the Cowes, Isle of Wight installation. It is capable of generating a peak output of 140 MW from eight Olympus sets, and illustrates the space saving properties of such a station. The space required to produce 140 MW from gas turbine generation would only have yielded 30-40 MW from a steam powered plant. Like the majority of gas turbine stations, it can be set in operation automatically by a telephone call. Maintenance work has been reduced to the absolute minimum, only one engineer being required on site to carry out the essential checks.

The Cowes station averages about 4 hours per week operation. Interestingly enough, it is used for peak lopping more often in summer than winter. The usual countrywide power variation from winter to summer is about 4:1. The Isle of Wight has the same variation, but the summer produces the greater load, mostly because of the influx of holiday makers which almost doubles the Island's indigenous population.

The first Olympus generating set to be sold overseas was supplied to the Sociedade Nacional de Etudo E Financiamento de Emprendimentos Ultramarinos, or SONEFE, the public utility for the city of Lourenco Marques in Portugese East Africa. It was believed to be the first gas turbine generating set installed in the African continent that was based upon an aircraft engine. Intended for peak lopping and emergency use, it was located on the site of an old steam-powered station on a bay known as the Bay of the Holy Spirit. Installation of the 17.5 megawatt set began in 1965 and work was well advanced when, in January 1966, cyclone Claude struck, causing much damage and many deaths in the region. For several days torrential rain driven by hurricane-force winds lashed the site, bringing all work to a halt. At the height of the storm, 6.5 inches of rain fell in one hour. Apart from flooding in some storerooms, no damage was caused to the installation, and it was duly commissioned not long afterwards.

While the Lourenco Marques power station was approaching completion, a second foreign order was received for an Olympus 17.5 megawatt generating set, this time to supplement a Proteus set already in use at Las Palmas, in the Canary Islands.

Following the acquisition of BSEL by Rolls-Royce in 1966, it was decided to concentrate all the industrial and marine activity at one site. So in March 1967 the Rolls-Royce Industrial and Marine Gas Turbine Division was formed, with its headquarters located at the old Bristol Siddeley Industrial Division premises at Ansty. W F Saxton was appointed as Managing Director, with W H Lindsay, previously Technical Director BSID, as Director of Engineering.

Orders continued to flow in, six Olympus sets being ordered for the Drax Power Station in the West Riding of Yorkshire in July 1967. Drax was planned to be the most powerful coal-fired station in England, and required an accordingly powerful peak lopping ability. By September 1970, the Central Electricity Generating Board had installed a total of 137 Rolls-Royce industrial gas turbines; 88 Avons, 42 Olympus and 7 Proteus.

In November 1970 an agreement was signed between Rolls-Royce and Allis-Chalmers Manufacturing Company of West Allis, Wisconsin for the production of electrical generating sets using Olympus gas generators and Allis-Chalmers electrical generating equipment. An initial contract valued at two million pounds was received for the first six sets. The Allis-Chalmers 100 was the first to be marketed, and consisted of three modules each comprising two Olympus gas generators, complete with power turbines, electrical generators, switchgear and control equipment. The set produced 100 megawatts in 100 seconds and occupied a site 100 feet square. It could operate either on natural gas or liquid fuel, and was capable of being remotely controlled.

A power station containing two Olympus SK30 sets nearing completion in Port of Spain, Trinidad. The urban environment set severe standards for the control of noise and pollution.

[*Rolls-Royce*]

An Australian contract for an Olympus generating set, received in 1975, was a one million pound order for an SK20 set site-rated at 15-16 megawatts for the Western Mining Corporation nickel smelter near Kalgoorlie in Western Australia. Following hard on its heels came an order for a complete gas turbine power station to be supplied to the Northern Electricity Authority of Queensland. Powered by an SK40 set, the twin Olympus installation was located at Mackay, Northern Queensland. The SK40 could operate as a single or twin installation, and this feature facilitated the construction, as the first gas generator was commissioned in May 1976, producing 17 megawatts, and the second was brought on line in March the following year, bringing the total output to 34 megawatts. The station is remotely controlled from the Board's Townsville headquarters 240 miles to the north of Mackay. Maintenance is usually carried out in two short periods each year, and the station is tested and examined every eight weeks or so. The average annual running is quite low, about 100 hours, with the highest so far being 400 hours in one twelve-month period.

During 1975 Rolls-Royce extended their range of generating sets by devising the SK20M Compact, intended for installation in situations where 20 megawatts were required but space and weight were at a premium. Based upon the standard SK20, the Compact had its intake, exhaust and ancillary arrangements redesigned to minimise space requirements, and was ideally suited to installation on oil platforms. The complete set was skid-mounted, and was designed to be completely packaged on land and shipped to an off-shore platform as a ready-to-use module. Its weight was about 170 tons.

In May 1978 Rolls-Royce revealed that it was developing an industrial version of the Olympus 593 (see Chapter 5), capable of powering a single-ended generating set in the 50 megawatt class or a double-ended set in the 100 megawatt class. It would have been available to contractors in 1980, but development was not proceeded with, presumably on the grounds that more modern engines such as the RB211 offered greater economy of operation.

Two SK30 Compact units that were to be the first off-shore Olympus generating sets were undergoing commissioning at Burntisland on the east coast of Scotland in March 1979. When commissioned and packaged, about the middle of the year, they were floated out by Conoco a distance of 500 miles to the North Sea's Murchison Field, and were installed on what was then one of the most northerly oil rigs to begin many years of reliable service. Another North Sea oil platform that makes extensive use of the SK30M Compact is the Brae A rig. Four generating sets are installed, three in constant use with the fourth on standby. Each set uses a three-stage power turbine driving a Brush electric generator. The principle fuel is gas from the Brae reservoir, but diesel fuel can also be used. The order for this installation was given to Rolls-Royce in 1980, after Marathon had evaluated a series of international tenders for the project. Later, an SK30 set was installed on the Britoil-operated Thistle platform.

A few days before the Queen made a state visit to Saudi-Arabia, in April 1979, flying there in an Olympus-powered Concorde of British Airways, two 20 megawatt Olympus-powered generating sets were handed over to the authorities. They formed the major source of power for the Military Hospital at Riyadh, one of the major stopping-points on the Queen's visit. In the same year, Rolls-Royce won a £28.5 million contract from the Egyptian Electricity Authority, which allocated full responsibility to the engine company not only for the gas generators but for all the civil engineering including fuel storage, switchgear and so-on right down to toilets and offices. The main generating plant consisted of four SK60 sets, which were located at Mahmoudiya, in the Nile Delta.

This installation near Kalgoorlie in Western Australia uses an Olympus SK20 generating set rated at 15 megawatts to provide electrical power to the Western Mining Corporation's nickel smelter. [*Rolls-Royce*]

126

This picture graphically displays the weather conditions in the North Sea—and this is a calm day. The Thistle platform shown is operated by Britoil, and has an Olympus SK30 set which was installed in 1983. *[Britoil]*

A remote jungle site for two **SK** 30 generating sets. Imiringi, in the heart of the Niger Delta, Nigeria. They operate on natural gas, a product of the oil fields, which was previously burned off. *[Rolls-Royce]*

As gas generator development progressed, it became apparent that the exhaust gases still contained a useful amount of heat after they had passed through the power turbine. This ultimately resulted in the principle known as co-generation, where the exhaust gas from the power turbine is fed through a waste heat boiler to produce steam. This is then used to operate a steam turbine to produce yet more electricity. In some subsequent installations hot water from the boiler could be directly used for space heating. Two SK30 sets were supplied to the Hague, in Holland, as a basis for a combined heat and power system, and were commissioned in 1982. A novel feature of the Hague installation was that the proportion of hot water to electrical power generated from the waste heat boiler could be varied to suit local conditions. Co-generation considerably raises the overall system efficiency, reducing to a minimum the amount of energy wasted.

The neighbouring Dutch city of Leiden became the second to operate an Olympus co-generation set in December 1986, when two SK30s were installed, to be operated by Energeibedrijf Rijnland (EGB). Shortly afterwards, an SK30 set was commissioned in Miami at the Dade County Government Centre. In the Miami installation, the power turbine waste heat gases are fed into a waste heat recovery boiler which can provide up to 10 megawatts of additional energy. The set is sited in an urban location, requiring particular care in meeting local environmental noise and pollution levels. The proximity of the Dade County Olympus generating set to the sea raised the possibility of salt corrosion, so special filters were installed in the air intakes. No salt accretions have been detected, but a fine sticky black powder gradually accumulates which has been found to be finely divided rubber, presumably from the tyres of vehicles using the high-speed elevated highway beside the plant. 1983 saw the start of an ambitious project in the heart of the Nigerian Delta. The installation had its origins in the fact that the oil fields in the region were flaring vast amounts of gas, and had done so since 1964. The installation of gas generating sets would utilise this wasted energy and provide electricity to a region of over 1,000 square miles containing approximately one million people in 90 towns and villages.

The area where the two Olympus SK30 sets were to be installed was a region where roads were few. It was swampy, infested with pythons, mambas and the infamous African Bee. The only practical form of communication was by water. The power station was sited near Imiringi, close to the Kola Creek Oil Flow Station.

Ansty had the responsibility for designing and constructing the entire power station and, in addition, had to engineer, provide and instal all the transmission lines, switchgear, substations and pylons. The site team, apart from building the power station, moved and placed in position some 361 kilometres of power line, held aloft by 5,000 one ton wooden poles and 12 metal pylons, 98 transformers and the building material to construct 100 sub stations at strategic villages throughout the state. The whole operation took five years, at an overall cost of £40 million. The complex was officially opened by Nigeria's Chief of General Staff, Vice-Admiral Augustus A. Aikhoma in June 1988.

Nothing lasts forever, and that is as true of gas turbine generating sets as anything else, so it is perhaps not surprising that the process of decommissioning Olympus sets has already begun. The first closures were at Ryehouse in Hertfordshire, and Croydon, in 1982. At the South of Scotland Electricity Board installation at Townhill near Dunfermline in Fife one of the 70 megawatt sets was decommissioned in 1985 and the other in 1986. Townhill was one of three twin-70 megawatt sets designed by BSEL in the early sixties, and had completed in excess of 40,000 hours of Olympus running at the closure.

Many of the Olympus sets in use will carry on into the nineties, and perhaps beyond. In 1989 Britoil awarded to Rolls-Royce a multi-million pound contract for the

Four Olympus SK30M compact sets on Brae A. Three are in continuous use with the fourth on standby.

[*Marcus Taylor*]

maintenance of an SK3OM generating set on the Thistle platform. The six year contract follows an earlier four year period, and signifies that Olympus operation in the North Sea will continue to at least 1995. To date the Thistle installation has clocked up over 30,000 hours.

Around 320 industrial Olympus-based units have been sold to 21 countries, accumulating over 1,500,000 hours of operation.

5. Concorde

The first review of supersonic transport in the UK was made at a meeting at the Royal Aircraft Establishment on 25 February 1954, but the real genesis of Concorde can be said to have been the first meeting of the Supersonic Transport Advisory Committee, (STAC), held on 5 November 1956 under the chairmanship of Sir Morien Morgan. Convened in London, the first meeting produced two clear proposals, a slender delta Mach 2 aircraft and a swept M-wing design for Mach 1.2. The committee considered all the aspects of supersonic flight, including the sonic boom, economics of operation, structural heating and so on, and on 9 March 1959 the chairman submitted the comprehensive STAC report to the Controller of Aircraft at the Ministry of Supply. It strongly recommended proceeding with two supersonic transports as soon as possible. One would be designed to carry 150 passengers over transatlantic ranges and would cruise at not less than 1200 mph (1.8 Mach Number) and the second was a medium range machine to carry 100 passengers over 1500 miles at 800 mph (1.2 Mach Number).

Feasibility studies were awarded to Bristols and Hawkers, the Bristol submission being the Type 198 which was powered by six Olympus turbojets in underwing nacelles. It was a 132-seater with an all up weight (AUW) of 380,000 lb and because it was considered to be too heavy, it was modified to 100-seat configuration as the Bristol Type 223 with an AUW of 250,000 lb, still with transatlantic capability.

In France, the Government-owned firm of Sud Aviation was concurrently studying a Super Caravelle, an aircraft with 1500 mile range and supersonic cruise ability, which also had Olympus engines. As the design contract awarded to British Aircraft Corporation (Bristols were absorbed into the partnership between English Electric and Vickers when that was formed as BAC in 1960) was conditional upon finding an international partner, and as the Americans were only interested in Mach 3, it seemed logical for BAC and Sud Aviation to pool their efforts. It took much burning of midnight oil for an agreement to be reached, with not a little government pressure exerted, but eventually on 29 November 1962 a treaty was signed in London by the Minister of Supply Julian Amery and the French Ambassador M. de Courcel. Significantly the treaty did not contain a break clause.

The UK was to have design leadership of the engines, as the Bristol Siddeley Olympus had been the original choice of both design teams, with a French engine company, SNECMA, being responsible for the jet pipe including reheat, primary nozzle and silencer. SNECMA, based at Villaroche in northern France, had many years experience in aero-engine design and manufacture. They had jointly developed silencers and reversers for Olympus engines in the fifties, and had produced, amongst other products, the highly successful Atar engine for the Mirage series of fighters. Sud-Aviation, based at Toulouse in southern France, was to lead on the airframe and to have 60% of the work. A host of equipment manufacturers were evenly selected in the UK and France.

An Olympus 593 on Number 140 test bed at Patchway, being prepared for a test run. An observation window can be seen on the left. [*Rolls-Royce*]

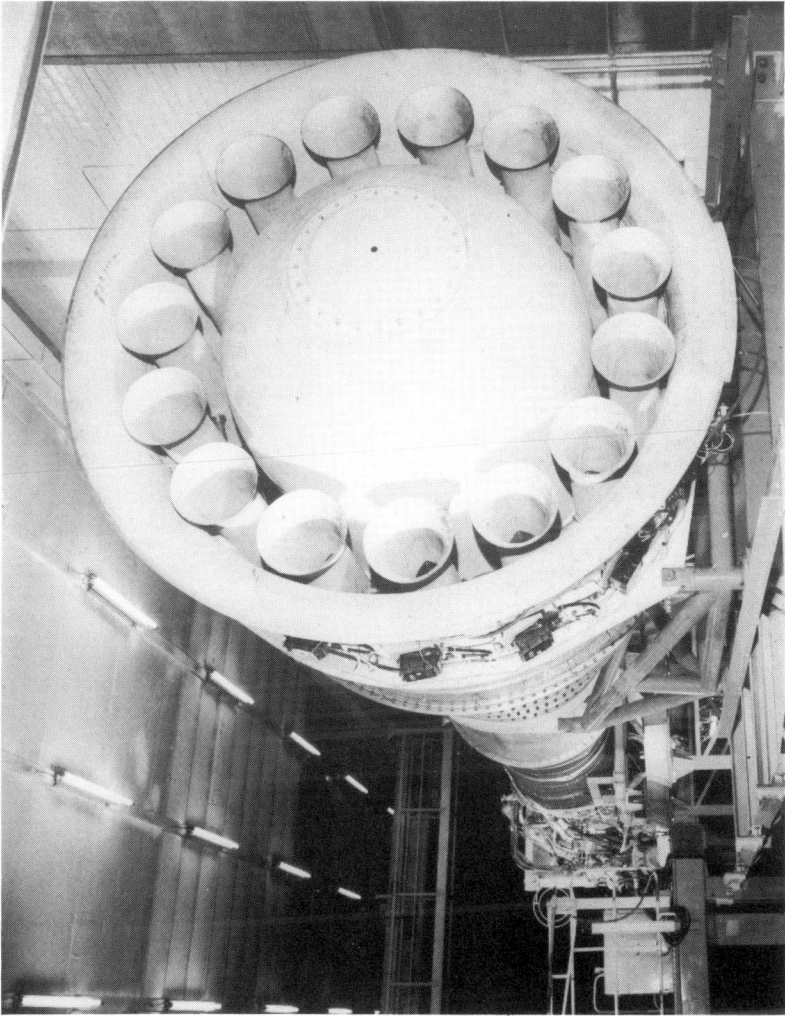

This device, which used 16 Olympus 101 combustion chambers, was used to pre-heat the air passing into the test engine in order to simulate the air intake temperature of 127 degrees centigrade experienced at twice the speed of sound—Mach 2.

[*Rolls-Royce*]

133

The crew of XA903 just before the first flight on 9 September 1966. Left-to-right, they are:- Jeff Wilson (now a captain on the Turbo-Union BAC 1-11), author, Tom Frost, Chief Test Pilot, BSEL, 'Harry' Pollitt, Deputy Chief Test Pilot, BSEL, Jean Beslon, Snecma flight test. [*Rolls-Royce*]

134

The initial design of engine for the SST was a civil version of the Olympus 22R redesignated as the 591. The 22R reheat system was deleted, and various detail changes made to achieve the overhaul of life expected of an aero-engine in commercial service. Progressive development to increase the thrust led to the incorporation of a cooled HP turbine, and a zero stage was added to the front of the LP compressor to increase the mass flow, the redesign being known as the 593. A variable nozzle was then added which in conjunction with compressors of improved efficiency and reheat formed the 593/3, capable of producing a take-off thrust of 28,800 lb.

Within twelve months of go-ahead being given, a major redesign of the aircraft was carried out to increase the operating range. This resulted in an increase in AUW which required a 12% increase in thrust, and although the 593 as envisaged had enough 'stretch' to encompass the increase, it would have eaten into the service development potential. As a result it was decided to completely redesign the engine around new compressors and turbines, the delay caused by this matching the corresponding timescale of the revised aircraft.

On 1 January 1964 the specification of the new engine was finalised. It was designated 593B - B for big - while the original design became the 593D, D for derivative. In the meantime, work was going ahead to build two 593Ds in order to gain early running experience. The first 593D ran at Patchway in July 1964, followed by the second in September, and at the second build one of them ran at 28,100 lb thrust, the highest dry thrust achieved by any turbojet to that date. One engine was retained at Patchway and the other was shipped to the French engine research centre at Saclay.

At Patchway the development programme covered a wide range of component reliability and environmental testing and in addition early experience behind a full size intake was gained. This was an important step forward, as it showed that the engine was capable of accepting the flow patterns created by a sharp edged supersonic intake. As well as starting three months early, the 593D achieved its design weight, the thrust was within 3% of target and cruise fuel consumption was within 1·5%.

140 test bed at Patchway was a purpose built facility for exploring engine behaviour at sea-level static conditions. It was linked by land line to the company's mainframe computer, which was another innovative step. A direct data link was also established between the Bristol and SNECMA computer centres so that rapid exchanges of test data and computed results could take place.

Heated intake tests were a vital part of the test bed programme, as it was known that at Mach 2 cruise the engine intake temperature would be around 120°C. The Bristol design of pre-heater used 15 Olympus 101 combustion chambers, a lovely example of 'keeping it in the family', and a similar type of pre-heater was operated at Saclay, using an Atar combustion chamber as the source of hot air. Use of a suction-type pre-heater meant that the Mach 2 cruise condition could be closely simulated on the sea-level test bed at a fraction of the cost of using an altitude test facility, or ATF. A simulated aircraft nacelle was also built to give a realistic air flow and heat transfer rate to the engine carcase. This used a complete 101, the exhaust from which would have been mixed with induced air at the engine intake. The 101 was operated in isolation, but never with a 593 behind it, as it was considered far too dangerous.

Since the primary nozzle remained choked during heated intake simulated cruise conditions on a sea level test bed, pressure levels and loads were adequately reproduced for the majority of testing. For part load testing however, such items as performance, handling, windmilling and relighting it was necessary to use altitude cells at NGTE and Centre d'Essais Propulseurs (CEPr), in particular the intake control laws were optimised

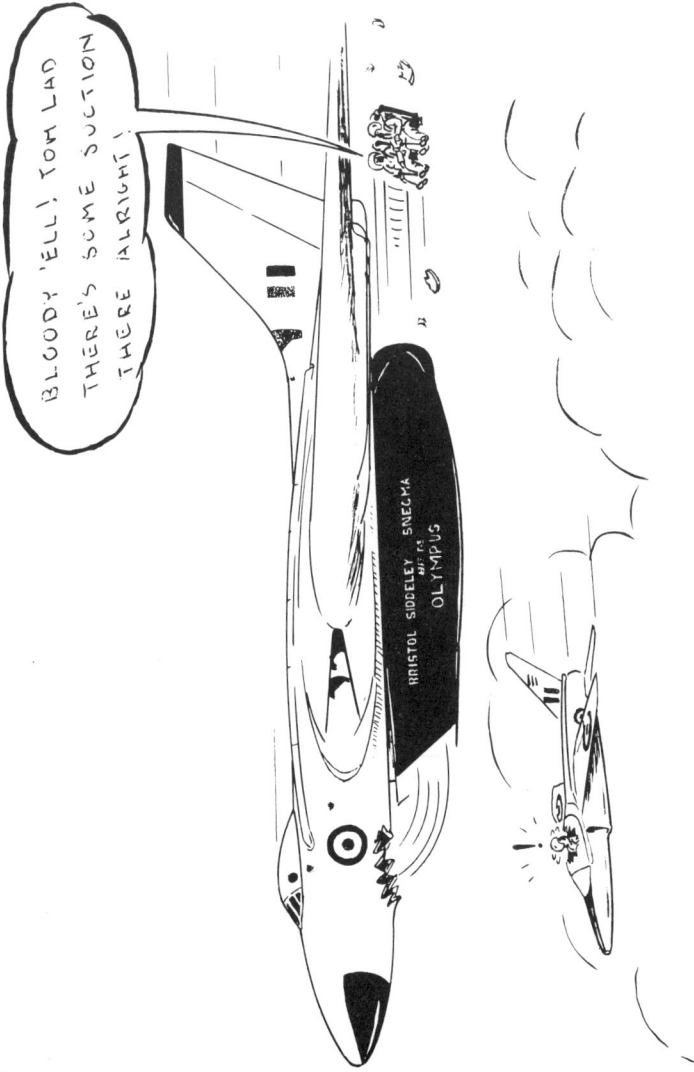

A cartoon that appeared in the Rolls-Royce newspaper at the time of the first flight of XA903 when it was thought that the suction caused by the high mass flow of the underslung Olympus 593 (400 pounds of air per second) would cause problems—it didn't.

[Rolls-Royce]

A clear view of XA903 from the Gnat chase aircraft, showing the water pipes leading forward to the water spray grid. The heavy staining on the Olympus 101 nacelles implies a considerable amount of breathing. [*Rolls-Royce*]

'Three greens for landing, intake ramp closed.' '903 on finals for Filton Airfield. The Welsh coast in the background implies that the Vulcan is on an approach to Runway 10.

[Rolls-Royce]

in Cell 4 at NGTE. Cell 4 had a free stream capability with 115% spill factor in the Mach 1.7 to 2.3 range at 593 cruise flows, and could also accommodate yaw or sideslip angles up to 4°.

At CEPr routine confirmatory checks on intake and nozzle performance were carried out with 1/10 and 1/13 scale models. A 1/3 scale twin nacelle was equipped with a representative intake control system to simulate supersonic operation. R5 test cell at Saclay was used for single-spool testing, extensive strain gauge investigations of the HP system over the complete operating envelope being carried out in the connected intake cell. In order to achieve the correct HP entry conditions, the seventh-stage LP stators were mounted ahead of the HP system inlet.

SNECMA at Melun-Villaroche also concentrated upon the exhaust system for the engine which comprised the afterburner, exhaust nozzle, thrust reverser and silencer. This testing included running a full scale primary nozzle assembly on an Olympus 301.

The 593Bs were phased out by mid 1966, the final test covering the operation of the rapid shut-down device. This was a 'running nut' on the end of the LP shaft. In the event of a rapid turbine acceleration caused by LP shaft failure, the device was designed to dump the fuel virtually instantaneously, thus minimising the overspeed resulting from such a failure.

The 593B was physically larger than the 593D. The diameter of the intake casing was about 2.5 inches greater and the engine was 10 inches longer. With a mass flow of over 400 lb/sec the dry thrust was 32,800 lb, increasing to 35,000 lb with the addition of the limited boost (9%) reheat system, which was largely based upon Atar experience. It had seven-stage LP and HP compressors, each driven by a single-stage turbine. The compressor casings were made of steel, and the drums and blades were fabricated from titanium with the exception of the last three HP stages which were made from Nimonic 90. The engine had the usual cannular combustion system with eight chambers. The HP turbine rotor and nozzle guide vane (NGV) assemblies had vacuum cast cooled blades, the LP turbine having solid vacuum cast stator and forged rotor blades.

Engine control was achieved by a two-lane analogue control system, both lanes possessing identical features. In the event of a failure in the controlling lane authority would instantly revert to the other, and this automatic transfer could occur in either direction. The policy that was eventually adopted for Concorde was to use each lane as the controlling lane on alternate flights, thus giving both lanes equal active running time and ensuring that dormant faults were not carried for more than one flight.

To achieve optimum operating performance, a jet engine needs to be supplied with air at a local Mach Number of about 0.5 at the engine face, and this should be maintained irrespective of whether the aeroplane is flying at low speed close to the ground or cruising at Mach 2 in the stratosphere. A simple intake cannot achieve this, as at supersonic speeds shockwaves, if not carefully controlled, can move down the intake throat causing severe distortion and loss of efficiency. The complexity of a variable intake is necessary to ensure that the engine is supplied with the correct amount of air at the correct Mach number at all times, in other words it ensures that the mass flows of the engine and intake are correctly matched for all phases of flight.

The Concorde nacelle was designed with a two-dimensional external compression intake. That is to say all the shockwaves generated by the sharp leading edges remained ahead of the intake, the velocity of the air being reduced to about 0.9 Mach number. The intake throat had a variable convergent-divergent section formed by the front and rear ramps, between which was an air bleed used to control the position of the shocks. There were four shockwaves, the last attaching to the lower lip of the intake and never

139

OLYMPUS 593. IN VULCAN F.T.B.

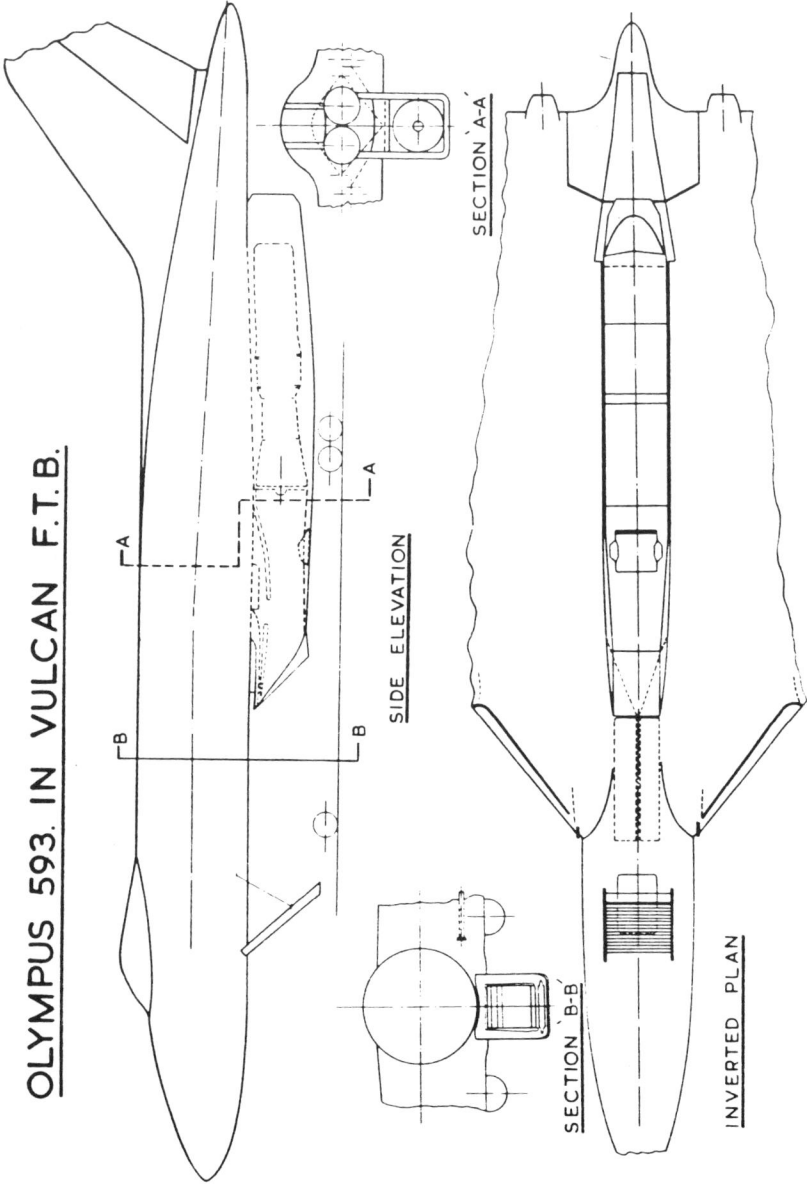

A

B

SIDE ELEVATION

A

B

SECTION A-A'

SECTION B-B'

INVERTED PLAN

This one is for modellers. It shows the arrangement of the single Olympus 593 nacelle mounted underneath the Vulcan flying test bed.

[Rolls-Royce]

Olympus 593s in the port nacelles of Concorde 001 at Toulouse, showing the way in which the engine dressing was literally moulded to fit the shape of the nacelle. [*Rolls-Royce*]

'Elle vol.' Concorde 001, the first prototype, climbs away from Toulouse Airfield on its maiden flight, captained by Andre Turcat, Chief Test Pilot of Sud-Aviation. 2 March 1969.

[*Rolls-Royce*]

inclining any further rearwards than the trailing edge of the front ramp. An auxiliary intake was fitted in the intake floor which also had the function of dumping excess air during periods of low engine demand. At supersonic cruise, the temperature of the air entering the engine was around 153°C.

Early in the programme it was decided that a flying test bed would be required to examine in detail the subsonic flight envelope, and Vulcan B1 XA903 was allocated for that purpose, arriving at Filton on 3 January 1964. XA903 had previously been used for early Blue Steel stand-off bomb trials at Aberporth on the Welsh coast and Woomera in Australia.

The conversion of the Vulcan took $2\frac{1}{2}$ years, and necessitated the fabrication of a nacelle which consisted of half a Concorde installation. This was mounted underneath the bomb bay which was filled with fuel and water tanks plus instrumentation and avionics. A simulated splitter plate projected forwards of the intake plane on the starboard side. In theory therefore the installation represented either a number one or three Concorde nacelle, but in practice it combined some features of all intakes.

The control system as initially fitted to the Vulcan possessed a single running line which defined the way that LP speed was varied as a function of HP speed. The first ground run of the flying test bed was completed in August 1966 and engine surge was encountered that prevented running above 80% HP speed. A control system modification consisting of a second running line parallel to the first but moved away from surge was eventually introduced, but the initial flights including the SBAC demonstrations were carried out with a maximum HP speed limit of 80%. The Olympus 593 flew for the first time underneath the Vulcan on 9 September 1966.

A wide variety of engine standards were flown, ranging from the early CS1 (Concorde Standard) to the -1, -2B, -3B Concorde first flight rating and -4, which was very close to initial production standard. It was planned to fly a 593-602 in the FTB, but the aircraft was required for tests on a different powerplant, and so the programme finished in 1971. Three different standards of auxiliary intake had also been evaluated as it was early realised that the initial 'barn door' type caused excessive drag. The aspects examined covered relighting, reheat operation, systems performance and LP blade strain gauging, in addition to which the gas turbine starter (GTS) was evaluated. Airfield noise was measured during flyovers but perhaps the single most important task undertaken was the anti-icing clearance. Carried out on the -4 standard, it resulted in a Special Category Icing Clearance being formulated for the prototypes.

To increase the flexibility of testing the two lanes of the Ultra control amplifier were frequently to different standards, permitting directly comparable tests. Control system optimisation occupied a large part of the flying. For example, the initial acceleration schedule assumed a rate of throttle opening that increased with throttle valve angle. Testing showed that there was a greater than expected surge margin at low rpms, and so the schedule was revised to a rate of throttle valve opening that began with a higher value and then reduced with increasing rpm.

The final and 219th flight took place on 21 July 1971. On the subsequent landing the brake parachute was streamed but failed to deploy, and the Vulcan made several circuits with the ragged remnants trailing behind it before a safe landing was made. A total of 420 flying hours had been completed.

Initial ground runs of Concorde took place in February 1968 at Toulouse and lasted three weeks, during which time a considerable number of teething troubles were overcome. The student unrest that swept France in the summer of 1968 delayed the next phase of ground runs, at one point the factory gates of the Sud Aviation plant at

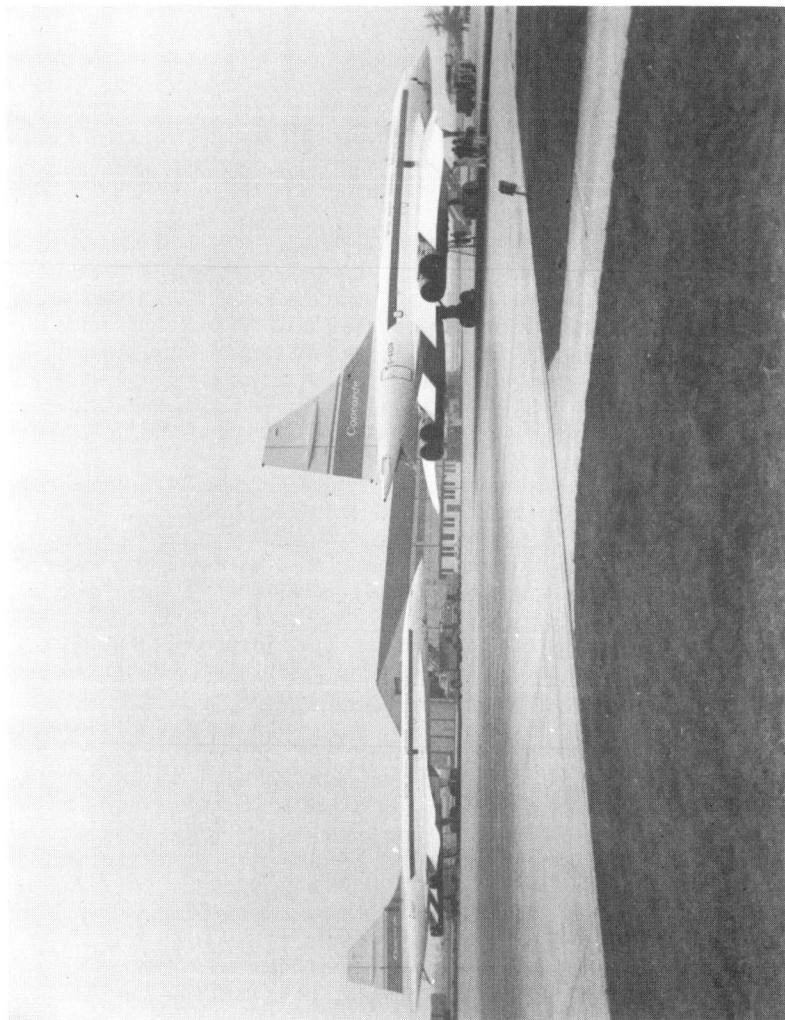

Concordes 002 (background) and 01 being prepared for test flights at the British Aerospace flight test facility at Fairford, Gloucestershire. 01 was a kind of half-way house, as it had the longer production-type front fuselage, but retained the prototype rear. [*Rolls-Royce*]

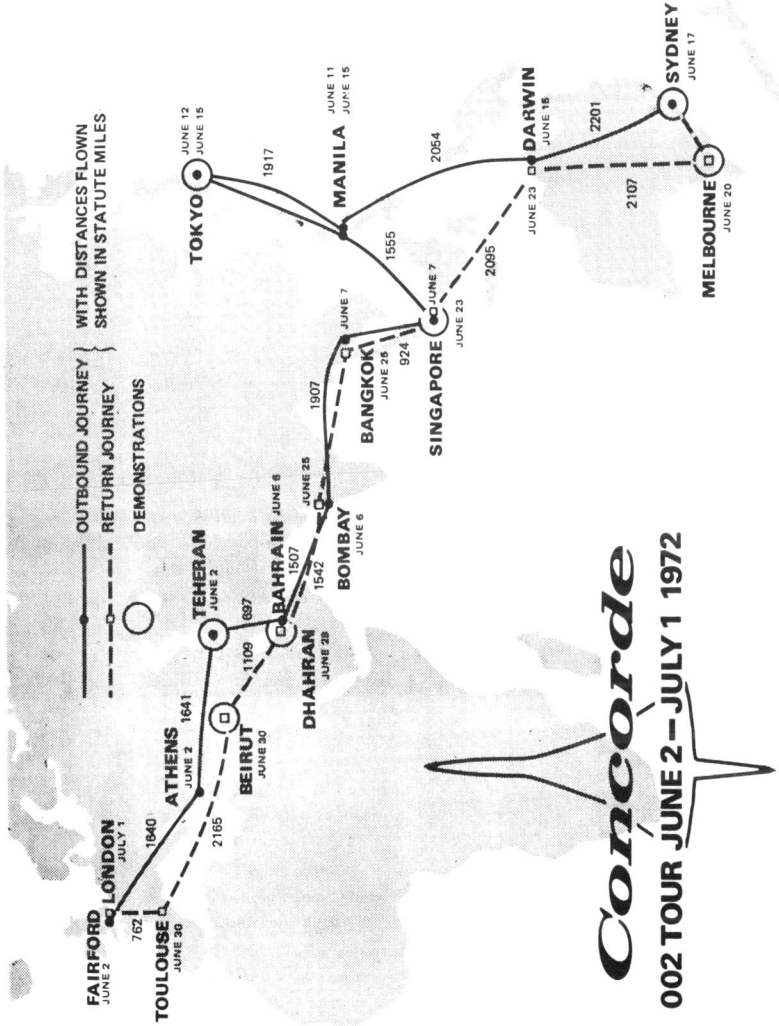

Concorde
002 TOUR JUNE 2 – JULY 1 1972

OUTBOUND JOURNEY ⎫
RETURN JOURNEY ⎬ WITH DISTANCES FLOWN
DEMONSTRATIONS ⎭ SHOWN IN STATUTE MILES

FAIRFORD
JUNE 2

LONDON
JULY 1

TOULOUSE
JUNE 30

ATHENS
JUNE 2

BEIRUT
JUNE 30

TEHERAN
JUNE 2

DHAHRAN
JUNE 28

BAHRAIN JUNE 6

BOMBAY
JUNE 6

BANGKOK
JUNE 25

SINGAPORE
JUNE 23
JUNE 7

TOKYO
JUNE 12
JUNE 15

MANILA
JUNE 11
JUNE 15

DARWIN
JUNE 15
JUNE 23

SYDNEY
JUNE 17

MELBOURNE
JUNE 20

762
1840
2165
1641
1109
697
1507
1542
1907
924
1555
1917
2054
2201
2107
2095

The route for the Far East Tour of Concorde 002 in June 1972.

[*British Aerospace*]

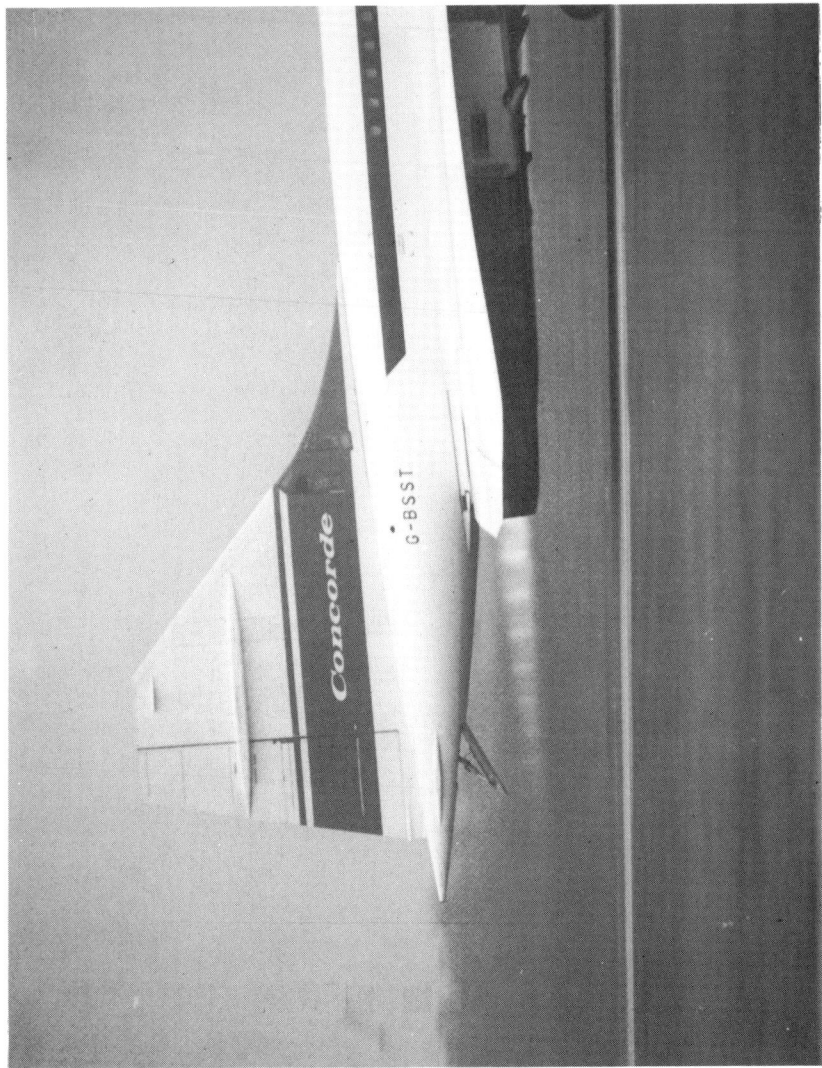

Concorde 002 takes-off from Fairford with reheat in operation. The auxiliary intake doors (prototype standard) can be seen at the right of the picture. The projection beneath the tail is the tail bumper.

[*Rolls-Royce*]

Far Eastern Tour, June 1972. Concorde 002 at Dhahran, on the Persian Gulf. These airport buildings must be among the most attractive ones ever built....

[British Aerospace].

...And these must be among the worst. Same tour, 002 at Manilla in the Phillipines, outside the burned out shell of the airport hall and control tower.

[British Aerospace]

148

Toulouse were welded shut. Another delay occurred when the door of the hangar that housed prototype 001 jammed partly open. It was reputed to be the largest up and over door in Europe and weighed about 300 tons; it had to be dismantled before the aircraft could be wheeled out.

The first flight of 001 with -3B engines installed took place on 2 March 1969. Carrying the French experimental registration F-WTSS and captained by Andre Turcat, Chief Test Pilot of Sud Aviation, the aircraft made a 42 minute flight during which it reached 250 knots at 10,000 feet. Several weeks later, on 9 April the British prototype 002 made its maiden flight in the hands of Brian Trubshaw. Registered G-BSST, 002 took off from Filton on a sunny afternoon and made a short flight to RAF Fairford, which was to become the base for Concorde test operations in the UK for the next 7 years.

From the engine point of view the early flights could almost be considered routine. Take-off noise was considered to be excessive very early, as for some reason which was never satisfactorily explained, the spade-type silencers failed to live up to their promise and the black smoke emitted from the engines earned the prototypes the unlovely soubriquet of 'Smoky Joe'. Both Concordes appeared together in public for the first time at the Paris Air Show in June 1969.

The task that faced the Concorde development team was truly daunting. The flight envelope was not only very much bigger than that of any other civil aeroplane, but the aircraft itself was a radical departure from the conventional layout, and the engines included reheat, a feature which will probably remain unique to the Olympus 593 for civil operation. An overall total of 4,000 hours was allocated to the flight test programme, split roughly equally between the two prototypes, two pre-production and some early production models. The bulk of the engine testing was carried out on 002 at Fairford. All the tasks were broken down in fine detail to ensure that, apart from certain confirmatory tests, no unnecessary duplication of effort took place.

The -3B engine standard used in the first two prototypes was rated at 34,370 lb, although for limited periods on test more than 40,000 lb had been developed.

There were several key milestones during the flight programme. The first flight was one such, as was the first supersonic flight which was allocated to 001, whilst 002 was scheduled to reach Mach 2 first. 001 went supersonic on 1 October 1969 and this was quickly followed by the first airline assessment of the aircraft, pilots from Pan American, TWA, Air France and BOAC flying at speeds of up to Mach 1.2. By February 1970 a 593 had demonstrated a life of 300 hours and on 25 March 002 went supersonic for the first time.

Concern over the effects of the sonic boom on old structures led to a series of measuring stations being set up on the west coast of Britain, and in September 002 made the first of 50 flights down 'boom alley', as the west coast route became known. The usual flight path for this was to head east from Fairford under the control of London Military ATC, then turn north up the east coast accelerating all the time to achieve the planned Mach number as the aircraft turned over the top of Scotland. The maximum Mach number would be held all the way south along the west coast. The final results were remarkable in that overpressure levels were low and far less damaging to buildings than the vibrations from passing heavy traffic. For each run down boom alley the crew were carefully briefed to avoid dropping a bang on Northern Ireland, which at that time had a particularly sensitive political situation.

On 4 November 002 made its first attempt to achieve Mach 2. While accelerating through Mach 1.4 at 40,000 feet a fire warning occurred on number two engine and the attempt was abandoned. During 002's flight 001 was airborne at Toulouse, and as

Active to the last, the final flight of the Olympus 593 Vulcan tested a revised reheat system. On landing, the braking parachute burst, and Tom Frost had to take the aircraft around again. He then had difficulty in getting rid of the 'chute. The 219th and last flight occurred on 21 July 1971.

[*Rolls-Royce*]

The size of the nearly completed Olympus 593 dwarfs the two workers, despite the fact that the engine has been partially lowered into its pit. [*Rolls-Royce*]

The damage to these blades was caused by a front ramp becoming detached at Mach 2, in Concorde 001. The engine suffered 100% compressor damage, but was still capable of attaining 90% of maximum rpm before surging.
[*Rolls-Royce*]

soon as news of the British failure was received, Turcat set off in a successful bid to reach twice the speed of sound. The fire warning on 002 was not genuine but simply the result of a hot gas leak, so a second attempt was made on 9 November. At 36,000 feet while accelerating through Mach 1.12 the number four Olympus lost all its oil, and had to be shut down.

On the 12th, with the oil leak rectified, 002 tried yet again to reach Mach 2, and after a long acceleration up the east coast and over the top the figure 2 eventually appeared on the digital machmeter. At 2.02 indicated Trubshaw gently reduced power and an enormous double engine surge occurred twice on the port side. As Trubshaw afterwards remarked, "I thought that World War Three had broken out". As the engine power had reduced the aircraft had slightly dipped its nose, and the wake from the wing leading edge had been ingested by the engines, with nerve shattering results. Later a redesign of the leading edge incorporating increased camber was fitted.

The 3Bs were somewhat short of thrust, which meant using reheat to attain high Mach numbers, the value of which depended critically on the ambient temperature. If it was 'hotter' than normal—ISA plus—then the aircraft would accelerate very slowly, sometimes being unable to achieve Mach 2. Engine surges continued to occur at high Mach number, the location depending simply upon which intake ingested the wake. The first engine shutdown at Mach 2 occurred on 7 December following a gearbox failure on number four engine. The intake spill system worked as advertised, and no buzz or instability occurred.

During 1970 the design of the production engine was finalised. Designated 593-602 it incorporated major changes. The inlet guide vanes were redesigned and reduced in number from 17 to 5, resulting in a 5% increase in mass flow. The familiar cannular combustion chamber was replaced with an annular combuster which contained sixteen vapourising tubes shaped in the form of a double walking stick, each having a fuel sprayer. The system has a pressure drop of only 2% and is virtually smoke free. BAC made a film about the modification entitled 'Concorde Gives Up Smoking'. The cast nickel alloy turbine blades had internal cooling on the HP rotor and NGVs. The simple reheat system had a single gutter and gave 22% thrust boost for take-off and 30% boost for transonic acceleration. The five main bearings were provided with squeeze film damping; this was the insertion of a thin film of oil between the outer track and the bearing housing to minimise the transmission of vibration. In addition the turbine bearings, numbers 4 and 5 were thermally insulated.

The secondary nozzle was also transformed into the TRA, or thrust reverse aft, configuration. This dispensed with the multiple petal secondary nozzle, replacing it with a bucket type which also acted as a thrust reverser, making a significant saving in weight and permitting better nacelle/wing trailing edge integration. The 602 also introduced the lightweight fuel system which incorporated an air driven turbo-pump which was first flight tested on the Vulcan.

In January 1971 the first 100 supersonic flights were logged and on the 27th of that month a major incident occurred which demonstrated how tough the Olympus was.

001 was engaged in deliberate surge testing at Mach 2 to determine the engine handling boundaries. On flight 122 reheat was in operation on engines 1 and 3. When number three reheat was cancelled the engine oversped and surged, followed immediately by an interactive surge in number four. The surge overpressures in the number four intake were strong enough to cause a front ramp drive coupling to fail, which in turn was followed by the failure of the two final actuating links and the ramp hinge. The ramp broke free and caused severe damage to the intake before being blown out. Pieces

OLYMPUS 593

PRODUCTION

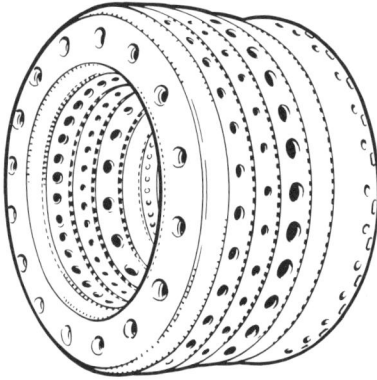

Annular Chamber

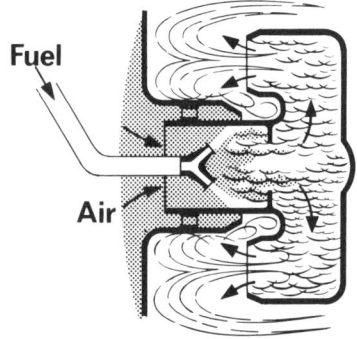

Fuel Vaporiser

PROTOTYPE

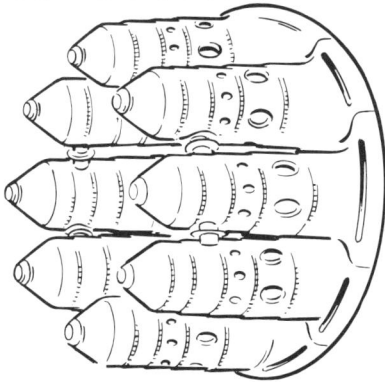

Cannular Chamber

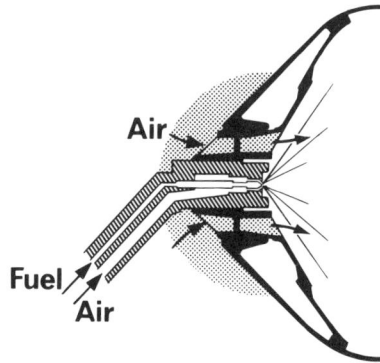

Fuel Atomiser

One of the most important changes between the development and production Olympus engines was the improvement to the combustion chamber. The reduction in smoke that resulted led British Airways to make a film entitled 'Concorde Gives Up Smoking'. *[Rolls-Royce]*

Civil Aviation Authority

Engine Type Certificate

for

ROLLS-ROYCE/SNECMA OLYMPUS 593 MARK 610-14-28

This is to Certify that the type of engine, together with any variants, named in this certificate is accepted as complying with the Airworthiness Standards specified in the Engine Type Certificate Data Sheet

[signature]

for the Civil Aviation Authority

Serial Number   SST1   Date   29 SEPTEMBER 1975

AD 206G

This document made the Olympus 593 Mark 610 the first ever civil turbojet to be certified for the carrying of fare-paying passengers at supersonic speeds.   [*Rolls-Royce*]

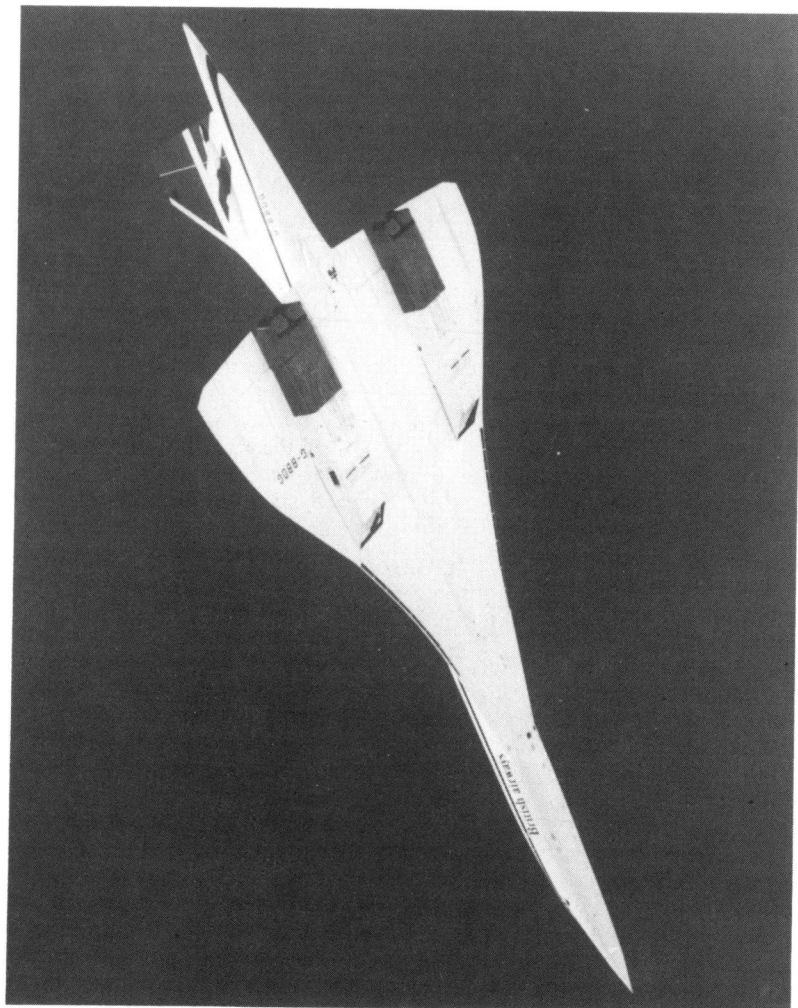

Concorde 202, G-BBDG, which carried out a large part of the production engine testing, operating from Fairford and Filton airfields. The first British-built production-standard aircraft, it never went into service. It is still at Filton, kept in a specially-built hangar, and is now used as a source of spares.   [Rolls-Royce]

156

of metal of varying size were ingested by the engine, which was promptly shut down after multiple surges. At Mach 1.2 during the aircraft deceleration it was restarted, and it attained 90% before surging. At that point a visual examination through the periscope showed that the front ramp was missing, and the engine was shut down again.

On the ground the full extent of the damage could be seen. The departure of the front ramp had resulted in very heavy engine damage. Every blade on the LP and HP compressors was damaged, as were the HP turbine rotor blades and NGVs. Only the LP turbine was considered salvageable. As the Flight magazine afterwards reported; 'Only the Olympus could swallow an intake ramp at Mach 2, suffer 100% compressor damage, and still be able to run at 90% HP rpm without surging.' The surges at Mach 2 were high energy events, and Rolls-Royce was particularly pleased by the results of the unplanned ingestion test.

001 was flying again remarkably quickly, and in May carried out the first inter continental flight to Dakar in West Africa. The 2,500 mile flight from the Paris Air Show took 2 hours 7 minutes. By July airline demonstrations were being given at Mach 2 and in August the 100th flight at Mach 2 was logged. From 14 to 18 September 001 made a trouble-free tour of South America. On 17 December 01, the first pre-production Concorde, registered G-AXDN, made its maiden flight from Filton to Fairford equipped with 593-4 engines and on the 21st all three Concordes were airborne simultaneously.

In April 1972 the first 602 engines were delivered to Toulouse to be installed in 02, the second pre-production aircraft and the first to have all the aerodynamic features of the production models. By this date the total 593 engine running experience had exceeded 20,000 hours, and by mid May 1,000 Concorde flying hours had been achieved.

The following month 002 left Fairford for a 45,000 mile sales tour of twelve countries in the Middle and Far East and Australia. The tour was supported by two RAF transport aircraft, a VC10 for the technical staff and a Belfast which carried two spare engines plus other equipment all the way around the world and back. The only problem with the engines was some minor foreign object damage which necessitated some experts being flown out from the UK to carry out borescope checks in, I think, Melbourne.

In August 1972 01 was returned to Filton to be brought up to full production standard including the fitting of 602s, and in September 002 appeared daily at the SBAC show and made several 'show the people' flights to various parts of the UK.

When testing multi-engined aircraft it is customary to instrument one pair of engines and assume that the other pair are symmetrical, that is that they will behave in a similar manner. The custom grew up of instrumenting the port pair, and this was followed when the Concorde LP compressor blade strain gauge programme was defined. The prototypes and pre-production aircraft were all cleared in this manner, but the assumption was found to be invalid on the production aircraft.

Measurements in the port intakes of aircraft 2 with the auxiliary vane intake door showed an effect on the first stage blades of the 602 which were vibrating at high power. This led to a check of the starboard engines and measurements showed that the number four engine had a high level of vibration at speeds below 60 knots. Intake studies showed that it was not possible to easily modify the intake, so a control system modification was introduced. The control amplifiers for number four engine incorporated an LP speed depressed datum of 88% which was invoked until the aircraft speed exceeded 60 knots, when the rpm was automatically allowed to rise to the take off value.

The latest mark of engine, the 610, was announced in 1973 and featured significant changes to the control system. The 610 demonstrated improved climb and supersonic cruise performance, and superceded the 602s as the production version. It was fitted in

OLYMPUS 593B POWER PLANT ARRANGEMENT

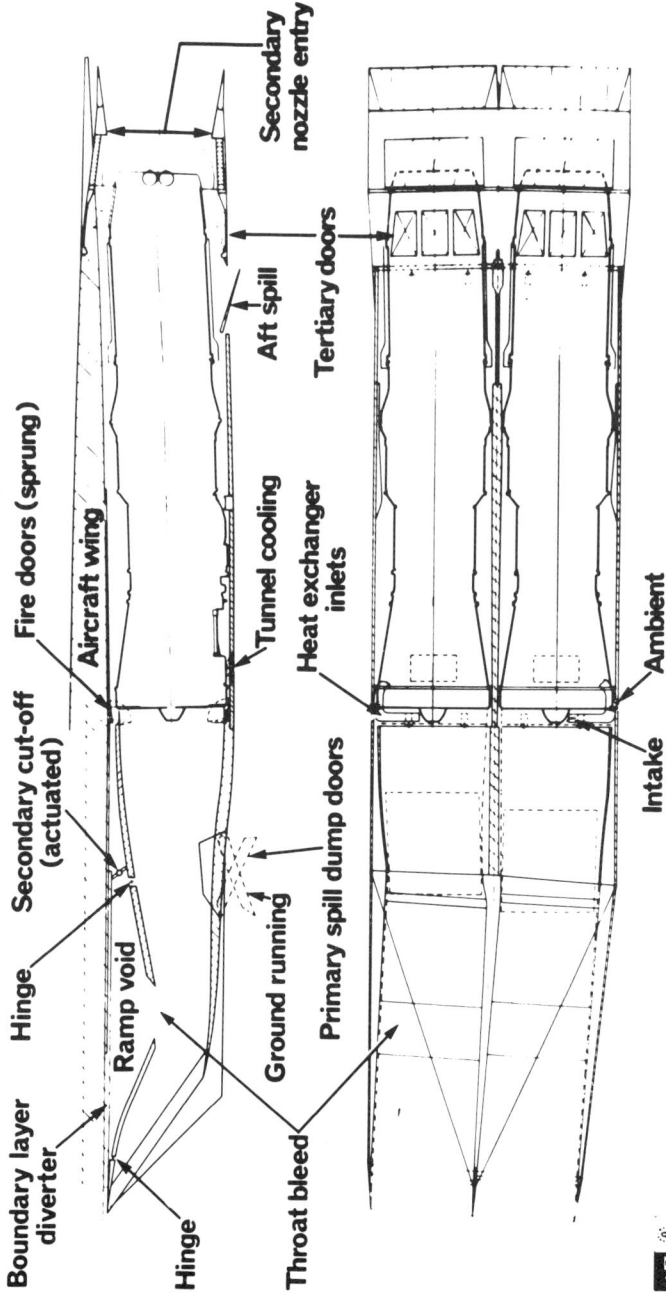

The layout of the twin-engined nacelles on Concorde. Most of this complexity springs from the necessity for efficient supersonic operation.

[*Rolls-Royce*]

158

all Concorde's from 203, which flew for the first time in January 1973. In June 001 and 002 made several high altitude atmospheric sampling flights in support of a series of international research programmes to improve knowledge of the stratosphere, reminiscent of similar trials carried out by a Vulcan B2 from Filton in the early sixties.

In the same month a flight of particular scientific interest was made by 001. A total eclipse of the sun was due, but the area of totality—from which the sun's disc can be seen to be totally obscured—lay in the Atlantic. If observed from a ship, the duration of the eclipse would only be 9 or 10 minutes, but if observed from a fast, high flying aircraft, the duration could be greatly extended. 001 took off from Las Palmas, and followed the track of the sun, staying within the zone of totality for 80 minutes, eventually landing at Fort Lamy in Chad.

The first flight to the USA followed on 18 September, 02 flying from Orly, Paris, for the official opening of Dallas Fort Worth Airport, with stops en route at Las Palmas and Caracas. The return flight to Paris from Washington DC was made in the record-breaking time of 3 hours 33 minutes. The increasing confidence shown in the aircraft was further demonstrated in December, when the first production Concorde made its maiden flight from Toulouse, reaching a maximum Mach Number of 1.57.

In 1974 a series of outstanding demonstration flights was made. In June 02 made the round trip from Paris to Rio de Janeiro, a distance of 12,000 miles, in only 12 hours 47 minutes as the climax to a series of route proving and reliability trials. Later in the month the advantages of supersonic speed were convincingly demonstrated. On 17 June 02 left Boston, Mass. at the same time as a Boeing 747 departed Paris, bound for Boston. Concorde flew to Paris, made a normal turn-round, and flew back to Boston, arriving before the 747.

In October 02 completed a very impressive American Pacific Coast tour, during which it visited London, Gander, Mexico City, San Francisco, Anchorage, Los Angeles, Bogota, Caracas, Las Palmas and Paris. To complete a successful year, 01 flew to Moses Lake in the USA on 7 December via Bangor, Maine, to carry out icing trials in natural icing conditions, making the fastest-ever civil crossing of the North Atlantic.

The first airline delivery was made to Air France, F-BVFA being accepted on 19 December 1975. A second, F-BTSC, followed on 6 January 1976, and the first delivery to British Airways, G-BOAA, occurred on the 14th of the month. In March an era came to an end with the honourable retirement of 002 to the Fleet Air Arm museum at Yeovilton. Initially kept in the open, a custom-built hangar was eventually provided to house a special Concorde display which included some of the aircraft that contributed to the programme, including the Handley Page 115 and the BAC 221.

Airline operation was started simultaneously by Air France and British Airways on 21 January 1976. BA flew aircraft 206, G-BOAA from London to Bahrain and AF flew aircraft 205, F-BVFA, from Paris to Rio de Janeiro via Dakar. On 4 February the US Secretary of Transportation, William T Coleman gave approval for BA and AF to operate two services per day each into New York and one per day into Washington for a 16 month trial period. The long battle against the anti-SST groups was over.

In the years that followed Concordes consistently operated at load factors of 80% or better. In 1978 the first charter flight proved an instant sell out, with many more applicants than there were seats available. Since then the special charter aspect of operations has proved a money spinner, as quite ordinary people are prepared to spend £300 to £400 for a one hour supersonic flight over the Bay of Biscay, and sample the superb Concorde cuisine. For many of them, it is the flight of a lifetime.

Two other airlines briefly operated 'the sharp ship'. Singapore Airlines agreed to operate a London-Bahrain-Singapore route jointly with BA in 1977, inaugurating the

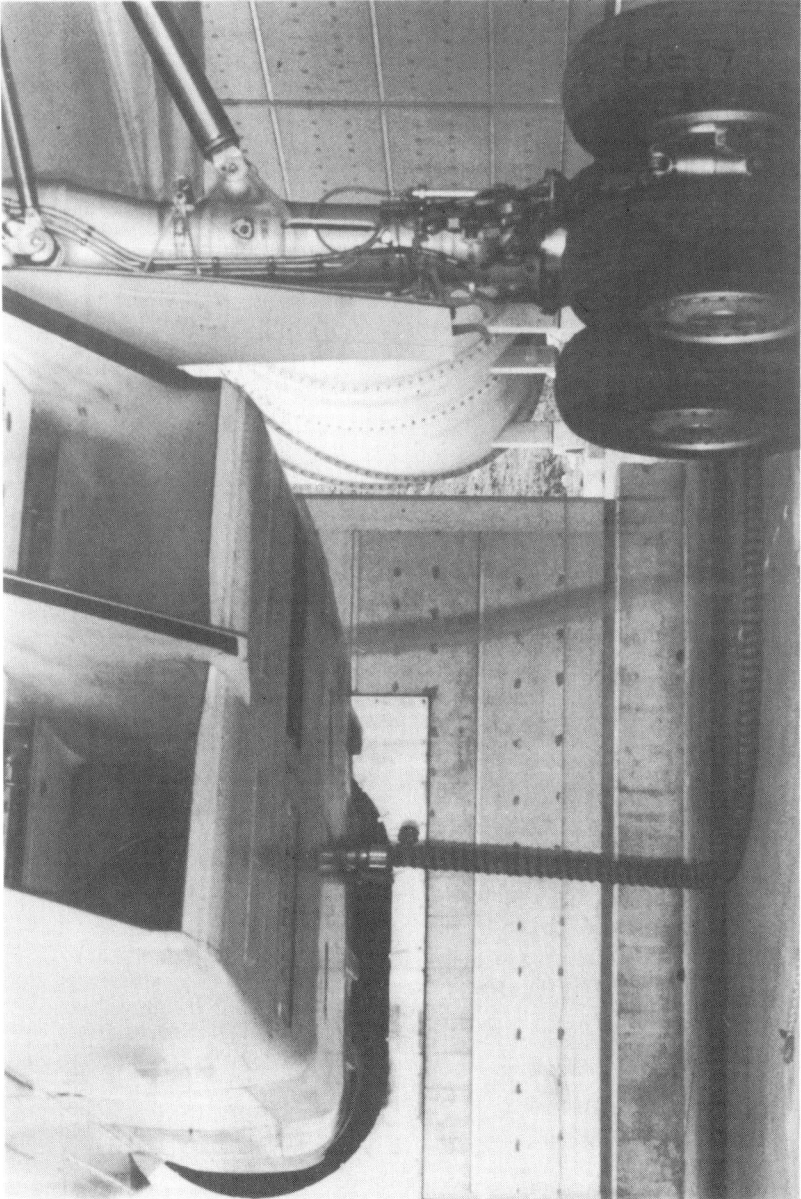

Concorde ground running in the silencer at London Airport. Only the right-hand engine is running, as indicated by the vapour in the intake. The humid conditions allow the vortex entering the auxiliary intake to be seen clearly.
[British Aerospace]

F-BFVA, the fifth production Concorde, in Air France markings. The exceptionally clean lines of the aircraft are shown to advantage in this view.
[*Rolls-Royce*]

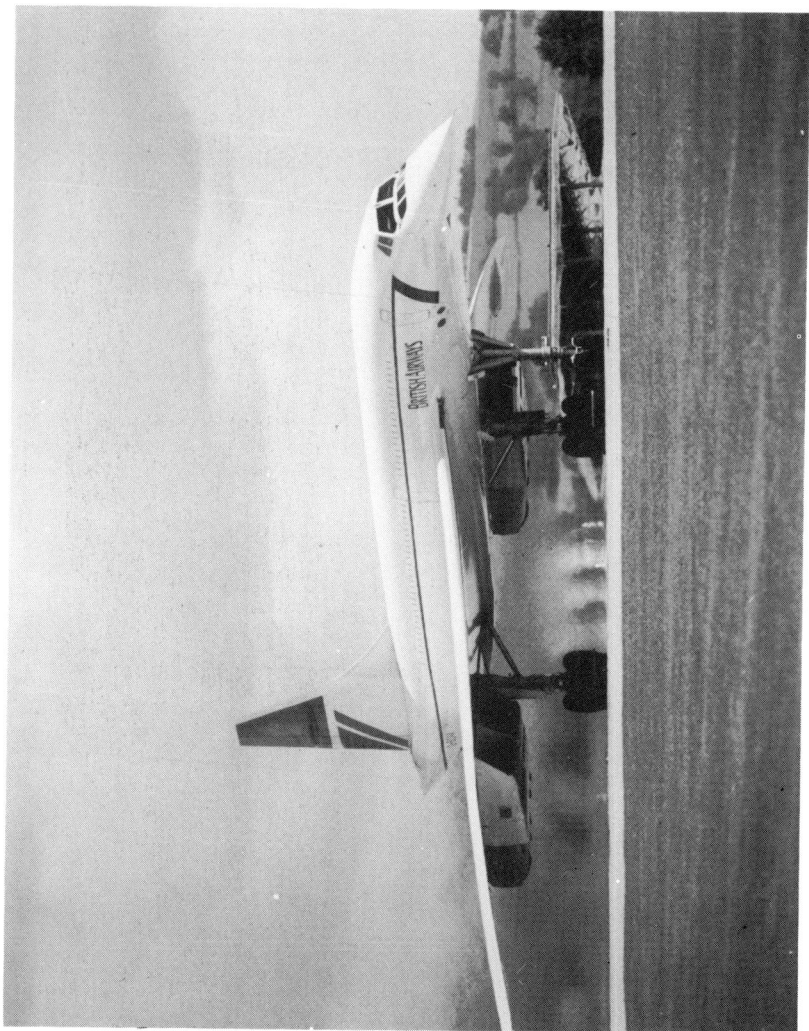

G-BOAA, the first Concorde for British Airways, prepares for take-off. The presence of the ski-jump in the right background suggests that the airfield is Farnborough, and the occasion the SBAC show.   [Rolls-Royce]

162

G-BOAG, the last Concorde accepted by British Airways, thunders into the air.

[*Rolls-Royce*]

Concordes were briefly operated by Braniff and Singapore Airlines, using aircraft belonging to Air France and British Airways, but supplying their own crews. This illustration shows G-BOAD painted—port side only—in the markings of Singapore Airlines.

[Rolls-Royce]

route on 9 December of that year. This service was suspended after only three flights whilst discussions were held with the Malaysian Government on overflying rights, finally being restarted in January 1979. The Paris and London services to Washington were extended to Dallas, Texas, the internal subsonic leg being flown by Braniff crews. For the US sector the aircraft had to carry an American registration. This was achieved by slightly modifying the European markings. For example, G-BOAA became G-N94AA, the G being removed for the Washington-Dallas leg. Neither service survived long, the Dallas flights finishing in June, and the Singapore flights in November 1980. This is not the end of the story, however. Even as these words are being written, a report in Flight International says that Richard Branson of Virgin Atlantic Airways has expressed a keen interest in buying or leasing two Concordes. Although a long term plan, his interests appear to favour two ex-Air France aircraft.

The Olympus has proved extremely robust in service, and very few serious mechanical failures have so far occurred, certainly none that imperilled the aircraft, but those that do are regarded with concern. For example, on 27 June 1981 British Airways Concorde G-BOAF was en route New York to London, established in the cruise at Mach 2 and 54,800 feet when a sudden violent vibration shook the aircraft. At the same time, fire warning, engine and nacelle overheat warning lights flashed on. All throttles were pulled to idle, and the auto-pilot disconnected. The number four engine compressor speeds were observed to drop to zero in a matter of seconds. This alone indicated a major failure, as normally the engine would 'windmill' if it was shut down. The aircraft diverted to Shannon where a precautionary landing was made. Examination of the number four engine after landing showed that the inlet guide vanes, the number one bearing and its housing were missing, presumably having been ejected through the intake spill door, thus causing the compressor to seize. There was also very heavy secondary damage to the engine and nacelle. The engine was replaced, and a three-engined ferry flight was made to London, where the aircraft was repaired and put back into service.

In 1988 the Olympus 593 reached a total of more than half a million flying hours in Concorde, of which half was at Mach 2, a figure that exceeds the combined supersonic experience of all the western world's military air forces. Since January 1976 more than 2.1 million passengers have been safely carried on scheduled services and charter operations.

Some of the achievements of Concorde are worth recording. The fastest commercial transatlantic crossing from New York to London took 2 hours 56 minutes in January 1983; the fastest flight speed between the same points was recorded at 1,490 mph with favourable tail winds in December 1985, and Concorde's longest commercial flight was 4,660 miles from Washington to Nice in September 1984. The maximum flight duration recorded was 6 hours 28 minutes, the longest supersonic cruise was 3 hours 7 minutes, the greatest height attained was 68,000 feet and the maximum Mach Number 2.23. A total of 144 Olympus engines were ordered and delivered to the airlines.

The current 610 rating of 38,075 lb thrust at take-off is only slightly less than the 38,275 lb thrust originally envisaged for the mark 621. It had been intended to progressively introduce the uprated versions as Concorde production proceeded, and the 621 would have been installed from the 41st aircraft onwards. A further uprating was planned to 41,360 lb, which was to have been achieved by fitting a zero stage to the LP compressor, and redesigning the HP spool.

There were numerous proposals for 593 variants to power stretched Concordes, advanced SSTs from various manufacturers and even a class of warplane known as a

The first British Airways Concorde shares a passenger terminal with several other types of aircraft. It shows that the 'sharp ship' required little in the way of specialised airport equipment. The early BA markings and the Vickers VC10 would date this scene in the late seventies.

[*Rolls-Royce*]

'supercruiser', which was intended to 'loiter' at Mach 2. They were mostly turbofan variants with bypass ratios varying from .07 to 0.95. Proposals were produced for Boeing, Douglas and British Aerospace. Most of the civil applications were meant to be quieter than the 593; they did not use reheat and produced more take-off and cruise thrust.

Olympus development may have stopped, but Concorde goes on. There is a saying in the aircraft industry; if an aircraft looks right, it is right. Anyone who has seen the grace and beauty of Concorde in flight will have no doubts as to the accuracy of that statement. After twenty years the gleaming white delta is still a conversation-stopper, for loved or hated Concorde is never ignored. Concorde's success is indissolubly bound up with the Olympus, which proved to be tough, adaptable and more than capable of the stretch necessary during the development period. I am sure that both will be operating well into the 21st century.

Grace and beauty in flight. Despite being more than twenty years old, Concorde looks as if it is fresh off the drawing board.

[*Rolls-Royce*]

GLOSSARY

AEO—Air Electronics Officer. Vulcan crew member who was responsible for the aircraft electrical systems.

Afterburner—A method of increasing thrust by burning fuel downstream of the turbines i.e. in the jet pipe. Very large thrust boosts can be obtained, but it is very noisy and has a very poor fuel consumption.

AUW—All Up Weight. The gross weight of an aircraft at take off, including airframe, fuel, passengers and freight.

Aneroids—A term used to describe those flight instruments, such as airspeed and altitude, that work by directly sensing air pressure.

Annular combustion chamber—An efficient form of low loss combustion chamber which produces very little smoke. It consists of an annulus into which the fuel is sprayed and then burnt.

AVTAG—A volatile aviation fuel. Also known as JP4.

AVTUR—A kerosine based aviation fuel, known as JP8, that has a higher ignition temperature than Avtag.

Axial compressor—A compressor which consists of a series of rows, or stages of blades arranged in sequence on a single shaft. Each row of moving blades is separated from the next by a fixed row of stator blades.

Boundary layer—The layer of air that is in close contact with a surface such as a fuselage or wing. Because of friction, this layer is slow moving.

BSEL—Bristol Siddeley Engines Limited. The Company that was formed by the merger of Armstrong Siddeley Motors Limited and Bristol Aero Engines in 1959.

Bypass ratio—The proportion of air that passes through the bypass duct of a turbo fan engine (see appendix) compared with its core flow.

Cannular—A type of combustion system which consisted of a number of combusters (also known as chambers or cans) enclosed within an inner and outer casing.

Capsule stack—A device used in fuel systems to balance one pressure against another in order to meter the fuel flow.

Centrifugal compressor—A rotary compressor in the form of a disc carrying vanes to accelerate the compressed air radially outwards.

Choked—A reference to the velocity of air through a narrow gap or orifice. It denotes that the velocity of the air has attained the speed of sound.

CODOG—CO(mbined) D(iesel) O(r) G(as generator). It means that the ship has both types of power plant, which can operate independently, but not together.

CODAG —CO(mbined) D(iesel) A(nd) G(as generator). A configuration where the diesel and gas turbine power plants can operate at the same time.

COGOG—CO(mbined) G(as generator) O(r) G(as generator). An all gas-turbine arrangement wherein the boost engines cannot be used at the same time as the cruise engines.

COGAG—CO(mbined G(as generator) A(nd) G(as generator). Used in the Invincible class of aircraft carriers, it means that any combination of its power plants can be used to propel the ship.

Combuster/Combustion chamber—Region of the engine where fuel is injected and burnt. Can be of several types (see annular, cannular).

Cross bleed—A method of tapping compressor delivery air from one engine to supply a service, such as operating an air starter to another.

COSAG—CO(mbined) S(team) A(nd) G(as generator). An interim design in which steam turbines and gas turbines could be used simultaneously.

Droop—A problem that affects some engine fuel control systems, where the RPM at altitude falls below the selected value.

Flutter—A type of vibration which can affect compressor and turbine blades in which they literally flap backwards and forwards.

Handling—A term used to denote rapid movement of the engine throttle lever. By convention, if the throttle movement between idle and maximum occurs in less than one second, it is known as slam handling.

HP—High Pressure

Hysteresis (throttle)—A problem caused by wear or play in the throttle linkage which manifests itself as a given throttle position producing a different RPM depending upon whether it is being opened or closed.

IAS—Indicated air speed

IGV—Inlet guide vanes. The fixed vanes that are visible at the front of an Olympus.

ISA—International Standard Atmosphere. An internationally agreed ideal description of the atmosphere in which the pressure and temperature at any height can be calculated by a mathematical formula, although the data is usually presented in tabular form. If, for example, the measured air temperature at a certain altitude is greater than the model, it is referred to as ISA plus.

Lock-in surge—A form of flow breakdown in an axial compressor which is self energising. The engine will have to be stopped and then restarted to resume normal operation.

LP   Low Pressure.

Mach Number—The speed of the aircraft expressed as a proportion of the speed of sound. The speed of sound is itself not constant, but varies with air temperature.

Overhung—A term applied to a compressor or turbine that projects beyond its support bearing.

Peak lopping—A technique used in power generation whereby peaks in demand are coped with by using extra generating capacity.

Power Turbine—An extra turbine placed in the exhaust from a gas generator in order to extract energy from the hot gases. It is mechanically independent.

Reheat—See afterburner.

170

Resonance—A phenomenon that occurs when the frequency of an applied force coincides with the natural frequency of oscillation of an object. (Hence the reason for a marching column of troops breaking step when crossing a bridge).

Slam acceleration—See Handling.

SSS—Self Shifting Synchronising. A form of automatic clutch which only engages when the input and output speeds are matched.

SST—Supersonic transport.

Stage —One row of blades in an axial compressor.

Stator—A row of fixed blades interposed between each row of rotor blades, which has the function of directing the air flow on to each succeeding row of blades at the correct angle.

Windmilling—The rotation of a compressor caused by the movement of the engine through the air i.e. a jet engine that is shut down in flight will rotate, the speed of rotation varying with its airspeed.

SHP—Shaft horsepower. A measure of the work extracted from the gas generator exhaust by the power turbine.

Surge (Margin)—A phenomenon that occurs when the smooth flow of air through a compressor breaks down. The resulting turbulence tends to act as a blockage; in extreme circumstances the air flow through the engine can reverse, drawing flame forwards from the combustion chamber. It has a number of causes, e.g. blade design, intake distortion, violent aircraft manoeuvring or too rapid engine accelerations.

The surge margin is the amount of leeway between normal operation and surge. The main task of the engineer is to ensure that the operator will not encounter surge in normal operation and the problem is complicated by the fact that the point of maximum compressor efficiency occurs just before the flow breaks down. The surge margin has to be large enough for the engine to be safely used, but not too large or there will be an unacceptable loss of efficiency.

TAS—True air speed. The true speed of the aircraft through the air, after all the installation and measurement errors have been taken into account. Used in calculation of mach number.

Uprating—The production of more power from an engine by allowing it to operate at higher jet pipe temperature/rpm.

Zero Stage—An extra compressor stage added to the front of the engine in order to increase the mass flow.

Appendix 1

Proposed Olympus Installations

Avro Vulcan Phase 6	B.01 23	4
Avro Atlantic	B.01 1/2A	4
Avor Type 740	Mark 551	3
Avro Design Study to OR339	B.02 21R	?
Bristol T172	B.E.10	4 - 6
Bristol T177	?	2
Bristol T180	?	2
Bristol T198	Mark 591	6
Bristol T200	Mark 551	3
Bristol T201	Mark 551	3
Bristol T202	?	2
Bristol T204 (OR339)	B.01 22SR	2
Bristol T205	Mark 551	3
Bristol T213	?	?
Bristol T223	Mark 593	4
DH (OR339)	B.01 14R, 15R	?
Handley Page 98	?	?
Handley Page Victor Phase 3	?	4
Handley Page 107	?	5
Handley Page Pacific	?	?
Hawker P1121	B.01 21B	1
Hawker P1129 (OR339)	B.01 15R	2
Gloster P370	B.01 6,7,7SR	2
Gloster P376	B.01 6,21R	2
Gloster P492/3	Mark 591	6
Martin RB-57F	Mark 701	2
Short PD45	BS127	?
Vickers VC10	Mark 555 with aft fan	4
Republic F-105 Thunderchief	B.01 21	1

Olympus Development and Military Family Tree

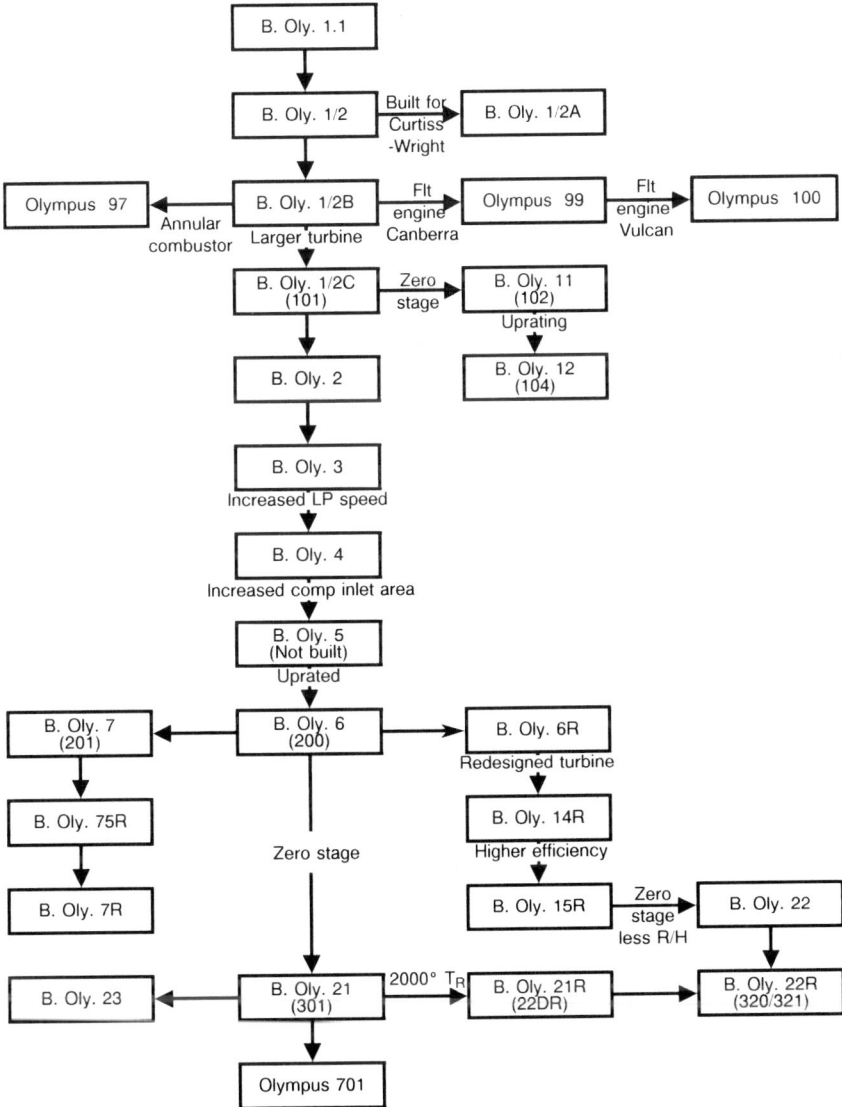

B. Oly. 1.1

B. Oly. 1/2 → Built for Curtiss-Wright → B. Oly. 1/2A

Olympus 97 ← B. Oly. 1/2B
Annular combustor | Larger turbine
Flt engine Canberra → Olympus 99 → Flt engine Vulcan → Olympus 100

B. Oly. 1/2C (101) → Zero stage → B. Oly. 11 (102)
Uprating ↓
B. Oly. 2 ← B. Oly. 12 (104)

B. Oly. 3
Increased LP speed

B. Oly. 4
Increased comp inlet area

B. Oly. 5 (Not built)
Uprated

B. Oly. 7 (201) ← B. Oly. 6 (200) → B. Oly. 6R
Redesigned turbine

B. Oly. 75R

B. Oly. 14R
Higher efficiency

B. Oly. 7R

Zero stage

B. Oly. 15R → Zero stage less R/H → B. Oly. 22

B. Oly. 23 ← B. Oly. 21 (301) → 2000° T_R → B. Oly. 21R (22DR) → B. Oly. 22R (320/321)

Olympus 701

XPIW244

Olympus Civil Family Tree (Simplified)

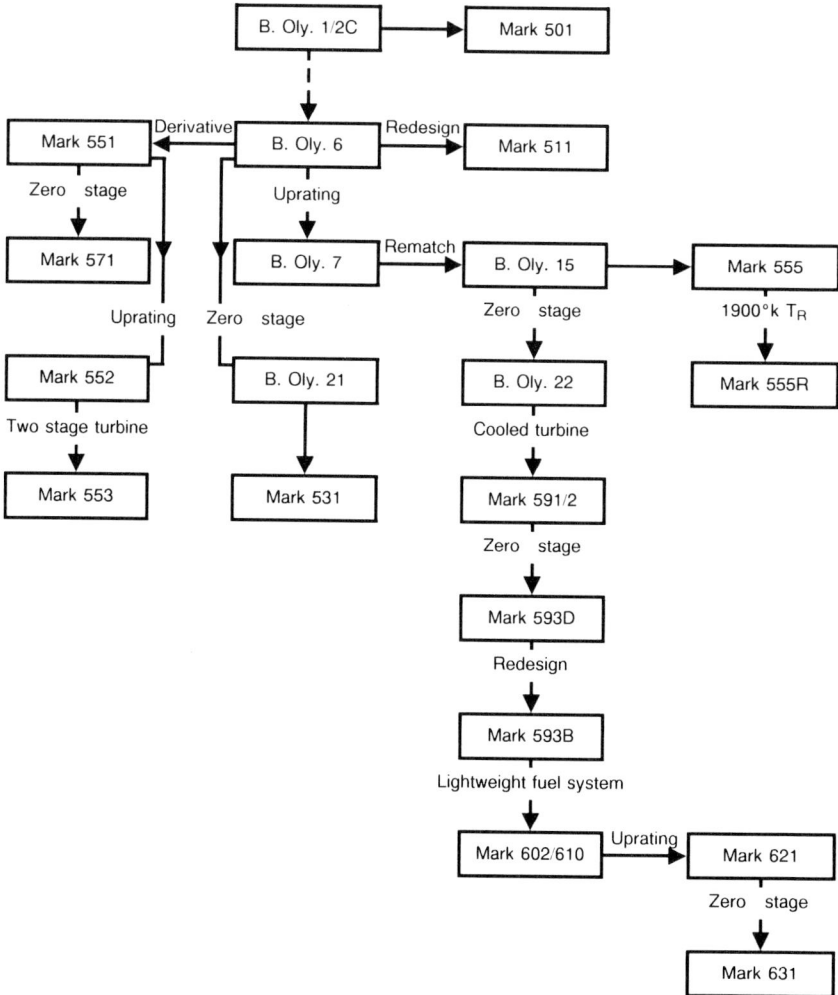

B. Oly. 1/2C → Mark 501

B. Oly. 1/2C ⇣ (dashed) B. Oly. 6

Mark 551 ← Derivative ← B. Oly. 6 — Redesign → Mark 511

Mark 551 — Zero stage → Mark 571

B. Oly. 6 — Uprating → B. Oly. 7

B. Oly. 7 — Rematch → B. Oly. 15 → Mark 555

Mark 571 — Uprating → Mark 552

B. Oly. 7 — Zero stage → B. Oly. 21

B. Oly. 15 — Zero stage → B. Oly. 22

Mark 555 — 1900°k T$_R$ → Mark 555R

Mark 552 — Two stage turbine → Mark 553

B. Oly. 21 → Mark 531

B. Oly. 22 — Cooled turbine → Mark 591/2

Mark 591/2 — Zero stage → Mark 593D

Mark 593D — Redesign → Mark 593B

Mark 593B — Lightweight fuel system → Mark 602/610

Mark 602/610 — Uprating → Mark 621

Mark 621 — Zero stage → Mark 631

BS Numbers		Thrust/sfc
BS 66	Olympus 555 with aft fan	20,923/0.479
BS 81	Olympus 591 with aft fan	25,190/0.465
		25,000/0.470
BS 81/2	Olympus 591 with aft fan	28,290/0.542
BS 81/3	Olympus 593 with aft fan	30,500/0.470
BS 81/4	Olympus 22 with aft fan	28.075/0.508
BS 100	Olympus 200 core	
BS 101	Olympus 22R derivative with PCB	36,000/
BS 102/2	High-bypass non-integral fan using Olympus 22 as gas generator	42,150/0.395
BS 127	Front split fan using scaled Olympus HP compressor	6,450/0.442

Appendix 3

Introduction

The principle of jet propulsion was demonstrated by Hero of Alexandria as long ago as the first century AD in the earliest 'steam engine' on record.

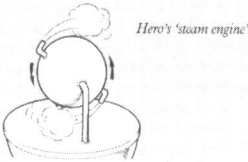

Hero's 'steam engine'

Equilibrium   REACTION   ACTION

However, the jet engine did not become a practical possibility until 1930 when Sir Frank Whittle patented the design of his first reaction motor suitable for aircraft propulsion.

The early jet engines were rather crude by today's standards, but development was rapid, and, though the gas turbine is traditionally associated with aircraft propulsion, it now has an ever-widening sphere of application, including ships, boats, trains, hovercraft, road vehicles, power stations and pumping equipment – all benefiting from the gas turbine's inherent qualities of high power, small size and low weight.

How does a jet engine work?

The gas turbine engine, commonly referred to as the 'jet' engine, is an internal combustion engine which produces power by the controlled burning of fuel.

In both the gas turbine and the motor car engine air is compressed, fuel is mixed with it and the mixture is burnt. The heat which results produces a rapid expansion of the gas and this is used to do work.

In the car engine the burning is intermittent and the expanding gas moves a piston and crank to produce rotary or shaft power which drives the car wheels.

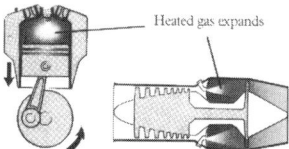

Heated gas expands

However, in the jet engine the burning is continuous and the expanding gas is simply forced out through a pipe or nozzle at the back of the engine – and confusion often arises, not so much regarding *how* the jet engine works, but *why* it works. It is often thought that it works by 'pushing' the exhaust gas against the atmosphere – but in that case how would a rocket engine work in the vacuum of space?

The answer is that the jet engine, like the rocket, works by *reaction*, on the principle expounded by the 17th century scientist Sir Isaac Newton – to every action there is an equal and opposite reaction.

Reaction can be demonstrated very simply by blowing up a balloon and releasing it. The 'power' which drives the balloon forward is the reaction to the compressed air being forced out of the neck of the balloon. When the balloon is inflated and the neck is closed, the balloon is in a state of equilibrium – the air inside is pressing equally all round the inside of the balloon; when the neck is released, the air inside, under the pressure produced by the tension of the rubber envelope, is forced out. The air flowing through the neck of the balloon is now in action, producing a reaction equal to it, acting in the opposite direction. It is the reaction on the front inner surface of the balloon which drives it forward.

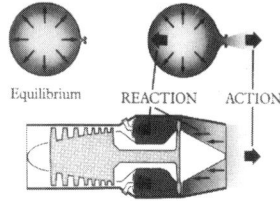

The 'hot end' of the jet engine can be regarded as the balloon. The reaction to the expanded gas being forced out of the nozzle acts on those parts of the engine opposite the nozzle, mainly the 'nose' of the combustion chamber and on the tail cone. The reaction – the 'power' of the engine – is transmitted from the engine casing to the airframe through the engine mountings, and is usually measured in pounds force (lbf), kilogrammes force (kgf) or the international unit, the Newton (N).

Layout of the jet engine

The jet engine is basically a machine for generating a large volume of gas which is forced out of the rear of the engine to produce a reaction in the form of forward thrust. The engine is therefore designed to collect a large volume of air, compress it, mix fuel with it and burn the mixture to produce the expansion which forces the gas out of the nozzle.

The engine has three main components – a compressor, a combustion chamber and a turbine.

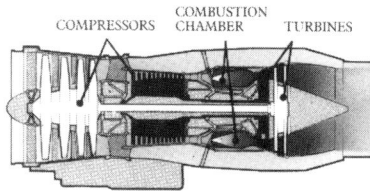

COMPRESSORS   COMBUSTION CHAMBER   TURBINES

The compressor

The compressor, situated at the front of the engine, performs two functions – it draws air into the engine and it compresses it before delivering it into the combustion chamber. Jet engine combustion will, in fact, work at atmospheric pressure, but efficiency and fuel consumption improve considerably when the pressure of the air is increased.

Compressors may be centrifugal and/or axial, the latter consisting of a number of stages of alternate rotating and stationary aerofoil-section blades which force the air through a convergent annular duct.

Many modern engines have more than one compressor because a high degree of compression requires a large number of compressor rows or 'stages'. Each stage has an optimum speed for best efficiency – the smaller the blades the higher the speed. If all the stages are on the same shaft, only a few of them will be operating at their optimum

176

speed – the majority will be running either too fast or too slow. This problem is overcome by dividing the compressor into two or three parts, each driven by its own turbine and each rotating at its optimum speed. By this means, compression ratios up to 30:1 can be achieved, resulting in extremely high efficiency and very low specific fuel consumption.

The combustion chamber

The air from the compressor section, at anything up to 450 lb/sq in, passes into the combustion chamber. This is an annular steel 'flame tube' or ring of tubes designed to achieve the most efficient combustion of the fuel/air mixture so that the maximum possible heat energy is extracted from the fuel in order to give the greatest rise in temperature and hence expansion of the gas.

The combustion chamber has a number of burners to vaporise the fuel before mixing it with the compressed air. Igniters are provided to initiate combustion. Unlike the motor car engine, combustion is continuous.

The turbine

As a result of the burning of the air/fuel mixture, the velocity and temperature in the combustion chamber increase rapidly and the gas is forced out of the rear of the chamber, through the turbine. The turbine consists of one or more stages of alternate stationary and rotating aerofoil-section blades. It is attached by a shaft to the compressor, and its function is to absorb enough energy from the gas stream to keep the compressor rotating at its optimum speed.

The complete rotating assembly – compressor, shaft and turbine – is carried on bearings and is known as a 'spool'. In a multi-spool engine, each compressor is driven by one or more turbine stages.

In the turbojet and turbofan, the turbine is designed to extract just sufficient energy from the gas stream to drive the compressors, leaving the remainder to provide the thrust. The turboprop and turboshaft, however, have an additional turbine which is designed to absorb as much energy as possible from the gas stream in order to drive the propeller or power output shaft.

The main types of gas turbines

There are four main types of gas turbine engine – the first two, the turbojet and turbofan, are 'reaction' engines, deriving their power from the reaction to the jet. The second two, the turboprop and turboshaft, operate on a different principle, where the energy in the gas is used to drive a separate turbine which is connected to a propeller or power output shaft.

TURBOJET

The turbojet, the simplest and earliest form of gas turbine, is used principally in high-speed aircraft where its relatively low frontal area and high jet velocity are advantages.

Examples are the OLYMPUS 593 in the Concorde supersonic transport and the VIPER in a variety of military aircraft.

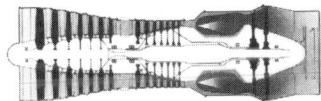

TURBOFAN

The turbofan is probably the most common derivative of the gas turbine for aircraft propulsion. It is a 'bypass' engine, where part of the air is compressed fully and passes into the combustion chamber, while the remainder is compressed to a lesser extent and ducted around the hot section. This bypass flow either rejoins the hot flow downstream of the turbine, as in the SPEY, or is exhausted to atmosphere through an annulus surrounding the hot exhaust, as in some versions of the RB211. In both cases the result is reduced overall jet velocity, giving better propulsive efficiency at lower aircraft speeds, lower noise levels and improved specific fuel consumption, features which make the turbofan ideal for both civil and military aircraft.

Examples are the RB211 in the Boeing 747, the 535 in the 757, the TAY in the Gulfstream IV and Fokker 100, the ADOUR in the Jaguar and Hawk, and the RB199 in the Tornado. The PEGASUS in the Harrier is a variation of the turbofan.

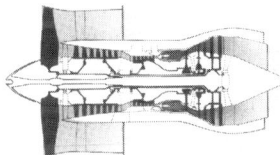

TURBOPROP

The turboprop is a turbojet with an extra turbine which is designed to absorb most of the energy remaining in the gas stream after sufficient has been removed to drive the compressor; in practice there is always a small amount of 'residual' thrust in the exhaust gases. The power-turbine drives the propeller through a reduction gear, usually at the front of the engine.

The turboprop is a very efficient power unit for relatively low-speed, low-altitude aircraft (eg 400mph/30 000 ft) though recent strides in propeller technology, in the pursuit of quietness and economy, have demonstrated the feasibility of a new generation of high-speed propeller-driven aircraft.

Examples of the turboprop are the DART in the BAe 748 and Fokker F27 and the TYNE in the Transall C-160 and Atlantic.

The power of this type of engine is measured in total equivalent horsepower (tehp) or kilowatts (kW) – the shaft horsepower (shp) plus the residual thrust.

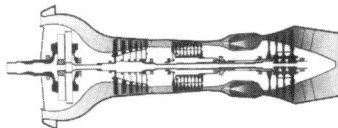

TURBOSHAFT

The turboshaft is virtually a turboprop without a propeller, the power turbine being coupled to a reduction gearbox or directly to an output shaft. As with the turboprop, the power turbine absorbs as much of the remaining gas energy as possible and the residual thrust is very low.

The power of this type of engine is normally measured in shaft horsepower (shp) or kilowatts (kW).

177

The most obvious application of the turboshaft is the helicopter, where the engine drives both the main and tail rotor, though turboshafts are widely used in industrial and marine applications, including power and pumping stations, hovercraft and ships.

Examples of the turboshaft are the GEM in the Lynx and the GNOME in the Sea King helicopters, and industrial and marine versions of the RB211 and OLYMPUS.

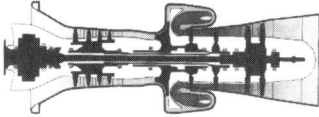

Variations...
Vectored thrust

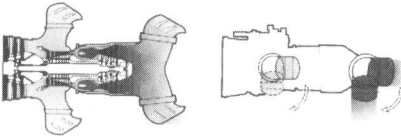

Thrust-vectoring is a means of changing the direction of the jet and hence the reaction or thrust in order to meet the requirements of V/STOL (vertical or short take-off and landing) aircraft. An example is the PEGASUS turbofan, which powers the Harrier, where the engine has four linked swivelling nozzles which direct the jet vertically downward for VTOL, through an arc to horizontally rearward for forward flight. In the Pegasus the fan or bypass air is discharged through the front two nozzles and the hot exhaust gas through the rear two.

Liftjets

Liftjets are very compact turbojets which are installed vertically in an aircraft to provide purely vertical thrust for take-off, hovering and landing. Liftjets are shut down during forward flight.

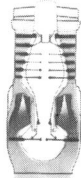

Ramjets

A ramjet is virtually a turbojet from which the compressor and turbine have been removed. Compression is achieved by the 'ram' pressure in the intake and for this reason the engine can operate efficiently only above about Mach 1 – the speed of sound. The ramjet has no moving parts and is the simplest of all air-breathing engines.

Additions...
Reheat

Afterburning or reheat provides a means of increasing thrust without increasing the engine's frontal area. Unlike a piston engine, the fuel in a jet engine is burned in an excess of air, so there is still a certain amount of oxygen present in the exhaust. These gases will therefore support combustion and it is possible to burn additional fuel in the jet pipe to increase the exhaust velocity and consequently increase the thrust of the engine. In a turbofan, where the bypass air provides even more oxygen, thrust increases up to 100% are possible by this method; it is normally applied to military engines for short-duration boost, eg for take-off or combat.

Reverse thrust

Thrust reversal is simply a method of altering the direction of the jet reaction, like thrust-vectoring, to meet an aircraft's operational requirement, in this case slowing the aircraft after landing. The jet deflection is achieved by three main methods; one uses clamshell-type deflector doors to reverse the exhaust gas stream; the second uses a retractable ejector to do the same thing; the third, used on high bypass ratio turbofans, uses blocker doors to reverse the cold stream airflow, which provides the majority of the thrust.

Pressures, temperatures and velocities

The following graphs show the changes in pressure, velocity and temperature of the gas as it passes through the various stages of the engine.

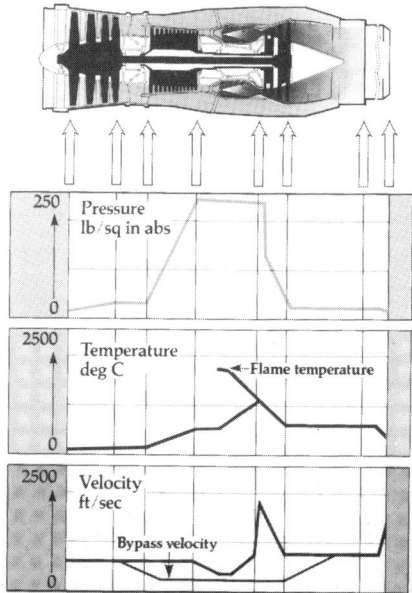

BIBLIOGRAPHY

50 Years of Bristol Engines. H.W.F.Bailey — Sales Publication Department 1970
V-Force. Andrew Brookes. — Janes 1982
Bristol Aircraft Since 1910. C.H.Barnes. — Putnam 1970
Flying Concorde. Brian Calvert. — Fontana Paperback 1981
V-Bombers. Bob Downey. — Arms and Armour Press 1985
British Aircraft Corporation. Charles Gardner. — Batsford 1981
Air War South Atlantic. Bill Gunston — Sidgwick and Jackson
The Murder of TSR2. — Stephen Hastings 1966
Not Much of an Engineer. S.G.Hooker. — Airlife 1984
Avro Aircraft Since 1908. A.J.Jackson. — Putnam 1965
Avro Vulcan. Robert Jackson. — P.S.L. 1984
V-Bombers. Robert Jackson. — Ian Allen 1981
Gloster Aircraft Since 1917. Derek N.James. — Putnam 1971
Hawker Aircraft Since 1920. Francis K.Mason. — Putnam 1961
Power for the Fleet. Christopher Preston. — Eton 1982
Project Cancelled. Derek Wood. — Janes 1986
Janes All The World Aircraft. — Various
Aircraft Engines of the World. Wilkinson. — Various issues 1954 to 1966.
Various issues of:- Aircraft Illustrated, Air Pictorial, Flight International, The Rolls-Royce Magazine, Bristol Siddeley News, Sleeve Notes, the Bristol RRHT magazine.
A Company brochure dated 1955 prepared for a possible agreement between Bristol Aero-Engines and Wright Aeronautical Division of Curtiss-Wright Corporation.
60 Years of Bristol Engines. G.M.Lewis. — Lecture 1980
Bristol Gas Turbines-The First Decade. F.M.Owner. — R.Ae.S. lecture 1962.
Marine Gas Turbine Experience in the Falklands War. Commander P.W.W.Ridley, BSc., M.I.Mech.E., R.N., Paper written in late 1982.

ROLLS-ROYCE
HERITAGE TRUST